Foundational
FAITH

Foundational
FAITH

Foundational
FAITH

Unchangeable
Truth for an
Ever-Changing
World

JOHN KOESSLER
general editor

MOODY PUBLISHERS
CHICAGO

© 2003 by
MOODY BIBLE INSTITUTE

Library of Congress Cataloging-in-Publication Data

Foundational faith : unchangeable truth for an ever-changing world / John Koessler, general editor.
    p. cm.
  ISBN 0-8024-2317-5
  1. Evangelicalism. 2. Theology, Doctrinal. I. Koessler, John, 1953-

BR1640.F68 2003
230'.044—dc21

                                                    2002155906

3 5 7 9 10 8 6 4

*to the students of
the Moody Bible Institute*

CONTENTS

ACKNOWLEDGMENTS

E very book is a group effort. That is especially true with this project. I want to express my appreciation to Dr. Tom Cornman, who originally conceived of the idea, selected the contributors, and then invited me to serve as general editor on this project. Thanks must also be expressed to each contributor for the effort they made to write under a difficult deadline and for their flexibility in responding to the sometimes painful work of editing.

Collectively, we are grateful to Mark Tobey at Moody Publishers for his support and enthusiasm for this project and to Jim Vincent for his patient and thoughtful work of editing.

INTRODUCTION

THE ESSENTIALS OF FAITH

About the time that D. L. Moody was settling in Chicago and beginning his work as an evangelist, Protestant Christianity in the United States began to wrestle with an important theological conflict. New approaches to science and history had begun to raise questions about a number of accepted beliefs of the church. Some within Protestant Christianity believed that the only way to keep Christianity from becoming irrelevant was to adapt its teachings and worldview to these modern ideas. Accepting contemporary theories about the beginnings of the world and biblical criticism, they called themselves "modernists."

Modernists abandoned belief in the verbal plenary inspiration of Scripture and the Virgin Birth, viewing them as preposterous in a modern era that had laid aside the superstitions of an earlier age. In a culture that was becoming more secular and rational, these "outmoded" doctrines had to be altered because they didn't seem to fit newer scientific models.

Within evangelical Christianity, a growing group of theological conservatives chafed at the thought of abandoning key doctrines simply because others had declared them unacceptable. They argued that these beliefs were found in Scripture, had been established by the ancient church, and had been universally held up to recent times. They were not about to see their churches change without a fight. In the beginning, their battles took place within churches and denominational schools on purely theological grounds. They claimed the doctrines being set aside by the modernists were "fundamental" or essential to the Christian faith.

The ideas they championed, however, did not begin with them. The propositions were rooted in the creeds of the early church and continued to be articulated through the Protestant Reformation. These ideas continued to find expression in John Wesley, Nicholas von Zinzendorf, and others in Europe who sought a return to the warmhearted piety of the early Protestant Reformation. From that time until the present, several key beliefs marked the evangelical brand of Protestant Christianity:

- a supernatural rebirth or a conversion experience,
- the Bible as God's revelation to humanity, altogether trustworthy,
- the mandate to spread the gospel at home and around the world, and
- the death and resurrection of Jesus Christ, which is what provides a saving relationship with God.[1]

A little more than a century ago, some members of the evangelical community began to stand up for the truths mentioned above, along with other fundamental doctrines, which they believed were essential to the Christian faith. They met in Bible conferences, started Bible institutes, and fought for the control of denominations because they believed that Christianity was at stake. Unlike the modernists, they believed that saving Christianity depended upon maintaining the supernatural elements of the faith—God's involvement in the affairs of man—that distinguished it from all other religions. They were convinced that to abandon these truths was to abandon the faith itself.

This conflict did not end with the close of the nineteenth century or the passing of the twentieth century. These truths continue to be challenged today by those who propose new doctrines, such as the "openness" of God, as well as by those who question established doctrines like the inerrancy of the Bible, substitutionary atonement, the existence of a literal hell, and the eternal punishment of unbelievers.[2] It is time for the evangelical church to reclaim Christianity's essentials and reaffirm our fundamental doctrines of the faith.

What makes Christianity different from Judaism or Islam— two other religions that claim the essential reality about God and life in general is found in divine written revelation? What do *evangelical* Christians believe that defines their faith? Are there essential doctrines or beliefs that, when absent, bring an end to the idea of a uniquely Christian faith? These critical questions deserve the attention of the church at the beginning of the third millennium.

This book is an attempt to reach back into the history of the Christian church and reclaim those beliefs that are foundational. As such, it is a book about ideas and theology. It is an attempt to think about the evangelical Christian faith from a worldview rooted in the belief that God is the center of all reality and it is His glory that matters most.

Not only is this book an attempt to think about theology from a distinctly Christian worldview, it is also an attempt to understand the evangelical faith at the beginning of the third millennium as part of a larger Christian discussion. We understand that as members of today's church, we are connected with a community of faith that stretches back over the millennia to the apostles. Our theology cannot be separated from the community of faith to which we belong. Our doctrine is rooted firmly in the divine written revelation of the Old and New Testaments—God's explanation of Himself to humanity.

Finally, a foundational faith is one that is focused on the person and work of Jesus Christ. Christianity without an authoritative Scripture and without the God/Man who saves from sin and provides redemption ceases to be a meaningful, potent faith. Instead, it becomes little more than another feeble attempt at solace and comfort without hope.

The five theological issues addressed in this book do not comprise an exhaustive list of Christian doctrine. They were chosen because they have been the focus of contention throughout the history of the church. They are the bedrock issues that remain the vital essentials of a biblical Christianity, regardless of denominational practice or polity.

These five doctrines—the authority of Scripture, the Virgin Birth, the deity of Christ, the substitutionary atonement, and the bodily resurrection and physical return of Christ—deserve to be reexamined by a new generation. The chapters that follow seek to elaborate and provide a contemporary context for these same core values.

Over the last two decades the leaders of the Moody Bible Institute (MBI) and other Bible schools have witnessed significant erosion of biblical and theological literacy among incoming students. We can no longer assume a basic knowledge of the story line of Scripture or familiarity with the core doctrines of orthodox Christian faith. Students entering our classrooms are struggling with what it means to say that Jesus Christ is God, that the Bible is inerrant, and that Christ's atonement for sin is the only way to God. Some have heard that God does not possess complete knowledge about the future and that those without faith in Christ will cease to exist rather than suffer eternal punishment in hell from spiritual authorities in their lives.

Some of our MBI students come from churches where solid biblical and theological teaching has been abandoned in an attempt to be culturally and intellectually relevant. We are in fact experiencing a new modernism, or more accurately, postmodernism, within the church. The clarion call of the gospel and the clear teaching of the foundational faith have encountered the clashing sounds of a therapeutic message of the mind and tolerant acceptance of the culture. This practice has resulted in the dumbing down of the Christian faith. Passion, in many instances, has overwhelmed knowledge. When it is not grounded in the authoritative teaching of Scripture, passion is often either misspent on things of little consequence or destructive to the cause of Christ. It is possible to be consumed with a zeal that is without substance.

We have written this book in an attempt to harness the passion of the current generation by providing the theological grounding necessary to direct and focus that passion in ways that will powerfully serve Christ and His church. Zeal is a dynamic force, and it is exciting to see it in the attitudes and actions of our students. It is our desire that this book serve as a compass pointing the reader in the right direction so that the enthusiasm already possessed can make a difference for the cause of Christ around the world.

With a desire to engage both head and heart, members of the Bible, theology, and pastoral studies departments of the MBI undergraduate school have joined together to present this introduction to the essential doctrines of evangelical Christianity. For more than a century, the Moody Bible Institute has been educating and training young men and women to be missionaries, evangelists, pastors, teachers, and lay workers who are capable of properly handling the Scriptures and understanding the fundamentals of the faith.

This work is not a complete theological treatise on the whole of doctrine but is designed to offer a starting point for discussion among the current generation of evangelicals. These great elements of the historic faith are the "base camp" from which we seek to advance the task of evangelical theological reflection. While there is more, much more, to consider and dialogue about, we have chosen to frame the discussion within the context of the rich history of a movement of which we are all heirs. It is our hope that we will keep their story alive, so that the next generation may also have fruitful discussion about what is essential and will be able to accurately proclaim the faith that was once for all delivered to the saints.

NOTES

1. Mark Noll, *The Scandal of the Evangelical Mind* (Grand Rapids: Eerdmans, 1994), 9.
2. Timothy C. Morgan, "Theologians Decry 'Narrow' Boundaries," *Christianity Today*, 10 June 2002, 18.

1

LAYING THE FOUNDATION

Thomas H. L. Cornman

I *believe in God, the Father almighty, creator of heaven and earth.*

I believe in Jesus Christ, his only Son, our Lord. He was conceived by the power of the Holy Spirit and born of the Virgin Mary. He suffered under Pontius Pilate, was crucified, died, and was buried. He descended to the dead. On the third day he rose again. He ascended into heaven, and is seated at the right hand of the Father. He will come again to judge the living and the dead.

I believe in the Holy Spirit, the holy catholic church, the communion of saints, the forgiveness of sins, the resurrection of the body, and the life everlasting. Amen.

THE APOSTLES' CREED

The Apostles' Creed centers on Christ. It declares Christ to be the only Son of God and Lord. According to J. I. Packer, the creed expresses with confidence the essential reality that "Jesus was, and remains, God's only Son, as truly and fully God as his Father is."[1] It declares that He was virgin born. His crucifixion, death, and burial were followed by His miraculous resurrection from the dead. It also affirms that this same Jesus who ascended into heaven will return as judge.

This preeminent creed was written to protect the church from theological aberrations and clarify what constituted genuine Christian belief. At the time, the fundamentals of faith were being challenged and even twisted. Today, as these fundamentals of faith continue to be challenged by those who propose new doctrines, we need to clarify anew what are the fundamentals of the faith and look at their implications for the twenty-first century man and woman.

BACK TO THE BEGINNING

When the early church began to carry the good news of salvation to the Gentiles, moving beyond the religious community of the Jewish people to whom the message of the death, burial, and resurrection of Jesus Christ had been delivered initially, questions soon arose. What was essential to the Christian faith? What necessary beliefs and behaviors were required for belonging?

Acts 15 records the first institutional discussion of questions. In the first verse we read, "Some men came down from Judea and were teaching the brothers: 'Unless you are circumcised according to the custom taught by Moses, you cannot be saved.'" This assertion led to significant discussion about the essentials of Christian faith and practice. The matter was so important that it could not be handled at a regional level. The disciples in Syrian Antioch sent a delegation to Jerusalem so that the matter could be concluded for the whole of the fledgling church.

At this early stage, the core question was soteriological: What results in the forgiveness of sin and the redemption of the individual? The apostles Peter and James both spoke to the issue, arguing that individuals are saved by grace through faith and not by adherence to external standards or behaviors. Both indicated that those who would add to faith were returning to the failed models of the past that neither earlier Jews nor the contemporaries of Peter and James could achieve.

The solution to the problem was clear. The apostles, representing the entire community of faith, declared that Gentiles should not be troubled by Jewish custom, but should be bound to the essential doctrine that salvation was by grace through faith in the Lord Jesus Christ (Acts 15:8–11, 19–20, 28–29).

They concluded that the central message of Christianity is the work of Christ on the cross, validated by His resurrection. Today, even those who would not identify themselves with *evangelical* Christianity acknowledge this: "Christianity is the only major religion to have as its central event the suffering and degradation of its god."[2] To that idea, the apostle Paul, in 1 Corinthians 15:12–19, adds that without the work of Christ on our behalf *and His resurrection from the dead,* we have a futile faith. The young church in Jerusalem understood this and protected her doctrine from the intrusion of contaminating elements that would have changed the message of life into a burden that no one could bear.

THE APOSTLES' CREED

The discussion of what constituted the essential elements of the faith continued after the New Testament era. Because the ancient world had a high rate of illiteracy, it became critical to find ways to protect the church from those who sought to alter the message of Christianity. The creed or confession became a defense against those with variant views who wished to gain a platform for their theological aberrations.

The Apostles' Creed represents one of the earliest attempts to provide such protection for the larger community of belief. The creed began by affirming the cardinal belief in God. This was not subject to debate in the early church. God exists and He is both all-powerful and Creator. The core of the creed was Christocentric. It declared Christ to be the only Son of God and Lord, born of a virgin. It affirmed His death, resurrection, ascension, and return to judge the world's inhabitants.

Implicit in the creed, although not clearly articulated, are two other important beliefs. One is the truth that Christ came to provide for the forgiveness of sins through His death. The other is the reality of a *bodily* resurrection both of Christ and of those who believe in Him. Consequently, four facets of the foundational faith were expressed either explicitly or implicitly in this third-century creed: the deity of Christ, His virgin birth, the substitutionary atonement, and His resurrection and return.

The perceived threats to the faith that had called for the Apostles' Creed in the third century led to a series of church councils beginning in the fourth century. The Christian faith began to gain popularity and eventually became part of the cultural mainstream during the time of Constantine when the persecution of the church ended. The preservation of the essential facets of the faith required increased vigilance. Roman culture had long been an eclectic mix of traditions and religions. In this environment Christianity was in danger of becoming commingled with other belief systems.

In A.D. 318, a church leader from Egypt began to suggest new ways of thinking about Jesus and His relationship with God the Father. He attempted to combine Christian theology with Greek philosophy and provide a simpler model of understanding a complex, abstract notion. Arius proposed that Jesus could not be the Father's equal. Instead, He must have been God's first and most glorious creation. He claimed that Jesus Christ was of a different essence from the Father and was not God.[3] The church exploded in response. The very foundations of the Roman Empire appeared to be shaken as well.

THE CREEDS OF NICEA AND CHALCEDON

In an effort to preserve both theological and political unity, the emperor Constantine called the leaders of the church together to engage in theological discussion. A council of the church met at Nicea to resolve the debate about the nature of Jesus and His relation to the Father. After heated discussion, another creed was formulated, designed to codify what the members of the council believed was the church's orthodox understanding of the faith. The Nicene Creed, as we know it today, sought to provide a standard against which those professing membership in the community of faith could be assessed.

The creed reiterated the substance of the Apostles' Creed with one significant addition. The full and complete deity of Christ was not clearly explicit in the earlier creed. To those present at Nicea, this lack of clarity allowed for Arius's views. The council decided it would eliminate the possibility of such an error in the future. The newer creed stated that Jesus Christ, "the Son of God, [is] true God of true God, begotten not made, one in being with the Father, through whom all things came to be."[4] The deity of Christ was upheld as a doctrinal essential in the fourth century and it was stated in a way that few could misunderstand.

The church continued to refine its confessional statements, as discussions about the person of Christ and His relation to the Father persisted throughout this ancient period. In each case, councils were called and definitions framed in response to novel approaches to doctrine that the church either had not anticipated or considered to be beyond the pale of orthodoxy. By 451, the church had convened its fourth ecumenical council to discuss the person and work of Christ. In this case the main question had to do with the relationship between the deity and humanity of Christ. A fifth-century monk by the name of Euty-ches was accused of teaching that Christ's humanity was fully ab-sorbed by His divinity.[5]

The Council of Chalcedon produced a definition that once again attempted to establish the boundaries of orthodox Chris-tology. The essentials included the Virgin Birth, the deity of Christ, and His work of salvation on behalf of a sinful humanity. The members of the council did not feel the need to restate the certainty of His return to judge. They did allude to the authority of Scrip-ture by affirming that the prophets of old and the Lord Himself taught in accordance with the content of the creed they produced.[6]

THE MIDDLE AGES AND THE REFORMATION

The church of the Middle Ages continued to define what doc-trines should be considered the irreducible core of the Christian faith. While there were a variety of theological opinions during this period, the Virgin Birth, the deity of Christ, and the belief in the authority of Scripture continued to be affirmed.

Contributions of Anselm

Toward the end of the eleventh century, Anselm, archbishop of Canterbury, England, wrote his landmark treatise *Cur Deus Homo (Why God Became Man),* which argued two essential points: God became man, and that man was Jesus Christ. For Anselm, Christ's full and complete deity was never in question.[7] Anselm's work also explained the reason why God had become man. The entire human race had sinned in Adam, leaving each person with a debt owed to God. Without satisfaction, "God can-not remit sin unpunished."[8] Someone had to provide satisfac-tion to God for man's sin. Since no human could make restitution for such an enormous debt, God had to become man in order to satisfy His own justice and bring redemption to human beings.[9]

We see in Anselm's writing the clear lines of the doctrine of substitutionary atonement, as opposed to the idea of Christ's death as a ransom to Satan. Anselm's treatise also alluded to the Virgin Birth and showed that he believed in the authority of Scripture.

Contributions of Luther

The Protestant Reformation continued the pattern of affirming the essential elements of Christian orthodoxy. Martin Luther, hailed as the first of the Reformers, was committed to the fundamental doctrines of an orthodox evangelical faith. Luther lived at the beginning of the sixteenth century and is credited with starting the Protestant Reformation in 1517, when he nailed his Ninety-Five Theses to a church door in Wittenberg, Germany. Paul Althaus, in his *Theology of Martin Luther,* described Luther's view on the atonement. He wrote, "Luther, like Anselm, views Christ's work in terms of satisfaction."[10]

For Luther, Christ made satisfaction for sinners in two distinct ways. He fulfilled the will of God through a life of obedience to God's Law, and He suffered on the cross as the punishment for sin by experiencing the wrath of God. In both instances, the benefit accrued to humanity and was done in our place.[11]

The first of the Lutheran confessions, Augsburg (1530), reflected Luther's commitment to the essentials. In this confession, all five of the core doctrines of the evangelical faith were clearly articulated. The authority of Scripture was affirmed in the preface and became the basis for all that followed.[12] The Virgin Birth, deity of Christ, substitutionary atonement, bodily resurrection, and return of Christ were also spelled out:

It is also taught among us that God the Son became man, born of the Virgin Mary, and that the two natures, divine and human, are so inseparably united in one person that there is one Christ, true God and true man, who was truly born, suffered, was crucified, died and was buried in order to be a sacrifice not only for original sin but also for all other sins, and to propitiate God's wrath. The same Christ also descended into hell, truly rose from the dead on the third day, ascended into heaven, and sits on the right hand of God, . . . The same Lord Christ will return openly to judge the living and the dead as stated in the Apostles' Creed.[13]

Contributions of Calvin and Knox

Like the Lutherans, John Calvin and those who followed him in the Reformed tradition tied their theology to the historic creeds that were compatible with their understanding of Scripture. In his *Institutes of the Christian Religion,* published in final form in 1559, Calvin expressed his positions on key doctrines. The Bible was authoritative, and as such it provided the foundation for the church and for her doctrines, rather than the Scriptures deriving their authority from the church. Calvin argued that the authority of Scripture must be determined through the inner witness of the Holy Spirit, rather than exclusively through the internal proofs in the biblical text.

Of Christ, Calvin asserted, "We indeed acknowledge that the Mediator who was born of the Virgin is properly the Son of God. . . . Although he was God before he became a man, he did not therefore begin to be a new God."[14] Calvin agreed with the position of Anselm and Luther, viewing Christ's death as satisfying God's justice.[15]

Calvin's influence spread throughout Europe and was carried to Scotland through the efforts of John Knox (1514–1572). He was responsible for the establishment of Protestantism in Scotland and for the formulation of a creed for the new church in 1560.[16] The Scotch Confession of Faith followed a Calvinistic view and touched on the essential doctrines of evangelical Christianity. Christ came in the fullness of time, being born of a virgin.

He was completely God and completely man, and the authors of the creed specifically denounced the doctrines of Arius and Eutyches, among others. This same God-man was crucified, died, was buried, and rose again from the dead. The confession affirmed that this resurrection was witnessed by many, including Christ's enemies. The reason for Christ's death was that He might voluntarily offer Himself as a sacrifice on behalf of sinful humans. This included suffering the wrath of God that sinners really deserved. Christ suffered in body and soul "to mak[e] the full satisfaction for the sinnes [sic] of the people."[17]

The authority of Scripture comes rather late positionally in the Scotch Confession. Despite its place, the confession follows the typical Reformed formula, expressing the sufficiency of Scriptures to reveal that knowledge of God to man that is essential for the Christian life. This authority came from God and not by church or council.[18]

The Westminster Confession

When the English and Scottish ministers met at Westminster in 1640 to create a new confession of faith for the English speaking kingdoms, they too came to the conclusion that the age-old standards of orthodoxy should be reaffirmed in the work they were producing. Since their confession was an extension of the Protestant Reformation, it must be understood as a reaction to Roman Catholicism and the prevailing fears that the monarchy was ceding ground to Roman doctrine. Nonetheless, the confession produced at Westminster was an attempt to articulate a clear and proper Reformed doctrinal standard. While the bodily resurrection of Christ was not explicit in the confession, the other four points were stated boldly. Scripture has authority and ought to be believed and obeyed. It is self-authenticating and because of that is to be received as the Word of God. Jesus Christ was virgin born and He is of the same essence as the Father and equal with God the Father in every way.

The ministers gathered at Westminster also committed themselves and their churches to the doctrine of substitutionary atonement. "The Lord Jesus," they wrote, "by his perfect obedience and sacrifice of himself; which through the eternal Spirit once offered up to God, hath fully satisfied the justice of his Father . . ."[19]

THE RISE OF MODERNISM

The views established during and immediately after the Protestant Reformation remained the core of evangelical Christianity throughout the seventeenth and eighteenth centuries. The Reformed confessions continued to be the general expression of belief. German Lutherans developed the doctrine of Scripture to a more complete level, building on the core "Scripture alone" concept of Luther. During the seventeenth century, Lutheran theologians began to explore the origin, inspiration, and authority of Scripture in depth. Luther and earlier Lutheran scholars had been content to take these areas for granted. Those who came later focused on the concept of verbal and full (plenary) inspiration; that is, the very words and the complete content of Scripture come from the Holy Spirit and are therefore authoritative.[20]

Presbyterians within the United Kingdom and the fledgling colonial church in America continued to subscribe to the Westminster Confession of Faith, which clearly articulated Reformed convictions. Those who abandoned some of the trappings of Reformed theology still clung to its core doctrines. John Wesley, credited with founding the Methodist Church, struggled with and finally abandoned some aspects of Calvinism. In doing so, however, he did not deny doctrines like the authority of Scripture, the deity of Christ, the Virgin Birth, the satisfaction theory of the atonement, or the bodily resurrection and physical return of Christ.[21]

However, two major intellectual forces shook the conservative evangelical world in the mid-nineteenth century and began to undermine the foundation of evangelical faith. Darwinian evolution and a scientific approach to understanding the Scriptures known as higher criticism began to make headway in American academic circles and from there began to filter into the churches. Neither concept was new. Yet both became viewed as significant threats to orthodoxy as more and more Protestants accepted these ideas and attempted to reconcile the Bible to them.

Evolutionary ideas had existed for some time in Europe and America. While the general theory of evolution had not raised significant concern among evangelicals, there had been some attempts to reconcile the new discoveries of science and the Bible.[22] Even C. I. Scofield, in an effort to explain apparent geological age, included explanatory notes in Genesis suggesting a gap theory of God's creative activities and incorporating the day/age theory in a footnote in his *Scofield Reference Bible*. The efforts of conservative Protestants to continue to reconcile science and the Bible was dealt a serious setback by the publication of Charles Darwin's *The Origin of Species* in 1859. The key issue was Darwin's introduction of the doctrine of natural selection to explain the basis of his evolutionary model. Before Darwin, most evolutionary theories had included the idea of intelligent design and progress in the upward ascent of the species. It was fairly easy for those who wished to maintain their commitment to conservative religion to see God's handiwork in an evolutionary model that acknowledged supernatural design and direction. However, by introducing a scenario that eliminated God's direct involvement (using the term "natural"), Darwin now proposed a theory antithetical to any view that attributed human origins to a supernatural source.[23]

The anxiety of early fundamentalists over Darwinian evolution had to do with what they perceived to be a bias against supernaturalism that lay behind the theory of natural selection.

Charles Hodge, writing in 1874, expressed the crux of the matter succinctly, "It is however neither evolution nor natural selection which give Darwinism its peculiar character and importance. It is that Darwin rejects all teleology, or doctrine of final causes. He denies design in any of the organisms in the vegetable or animal world."[24] The denial of design eliminated the supernatural and therefore ultimately ruled God out of the process. Hodge concluded that Darwin's theory disallowed supernatural revelation, miracles, and Christ's resurrection, and as a result destroyed the possibility of salvation.[25] This is what made Darwinism so pernicious to conservative evangelicals and would later kindle their backing of a spate of antievolution bills.

THE EFFECT OF HIGHER CRITICISM

Origin of Higher Criticism

Higher criticism posed an additional threat to evangelical belief during this period. An attempt to apply the scientific and historical methods of the period to the study of the Bible, it should be distinguished from textual, or lower, criticism, which primarily focuses on the accuracy of the transmission of the text of Scripture. The biblical criticism of that period focused on issues such as the authenticity of the text, identity and intent of the author, and the discovery of the chronological order of various underlying sources of the text.

The beginnings of higher criticism are typically credited to Jean Astruc, who proposed a documentary hypothesis to the Old Testament in 1753. Astruc argued that there were two underlying documents behind the Pentateuch, one for each of the names for God used in the text (Yahweh and Elohim).[26]

This method of criticism was carried to Germany, where it gained momentum and found academic respectability through the exposition of Johann Eichhorn. In 1780 he published an introduction to the Old Testament that reworked Astruc's theory and was widely accepted among European biblical scholars. Beyond the two original strands that he identified for the Pentateuch, Eichhorn supposedly found more evidence of multiple fragmentary sources for the first five books of the Old Testament. The work of German higher criticism found a home in Britain and the United States in the works of Bible scholars like Charles A. Briggs of Union Theological Seminary. In 1897, he published *The Higher Criticism of the Hexateuch,* which sought to employ the methodology developed in Germany during the course of the nineteenth century.

Impact of Higher Criticism

Like Darwinism, higher criticism as applied by liberal Protestants had a corrosive effect on traditional beliefs. Edgar Krentz provides a clear picture of the effect:

> It is difficult to overestimate the significance the nineteenth century has for biblical interpretation. It made historical criticism *the* approved method of interpretation. The result was a revolution of viewpoint in evaluating the Bible. The Scriptures were, so to speak, secularized. The biblical books became historical documents to be studied and questioned like any other ancient sources. The Bible was no longer the criterion for writing of history; rather, history had become the criterion for understanding the Bible. The variety of the Bible was highlighted; its unity had to be discovered and could no longer be presumed. The history it reported was no longer assumed to be everywhere correct. The Bible stood before criticism as defendant before judge. This criticism was largely positivist in orientation, imminentist in its explanation, and incapable of appreciating the category of revelation.[27]

Higher criticism led to an examination of the texts in a way that threatened the authority of Scripture. No longer viewed as "God-breathed," the Bible became a purely cultural creation, not very different from other similar writings of the same period.

With the authority of Scripture undermined, the key doctrines of the faith soon tumbled and resulted in the kind of theological modernism that the early fundamentalists characterized as "liberalism." Theological modernism emerged out of the social and intellectual climate of the mid- to late nineteenth century. It was marked by a strong anti-supernaturalism and a tendency to look at the Bible and Christianity through the lens of the developing ideas in the fields of historical and literary criticism, scientific theories, and comparative studies in the field of religion. J. I. Packer described the essential position of theological modernism:

> Liberalism maintained that modern literary and historical criticism had exploded the doctrine of an infallible Bible, modern science had made it impossible to believe in the supernatural as Scripture presents it, modern comparative study of religions had shown that Christianity, after all, was not unique, and modern philosophy required the dismissal of such basic biblical concepts as original sin, the wrath of God and expiatory sacrifice, as primitive superstitions.[28]

Theological modernism represented a divergence from the historic Christian orthodoxy that had marked the church since the Reformation and stretched back to the apostles. Liberalism no longer accepted the age-old message of supernatural redemption of sinners by God's sovereign grace. It rejected the grace of God and replaced it with nature. Liberalism took the divine written revelation and reduced it to mere human reflection. The central doctrine of faith alone in Christ alone was replaced by the belief that He had come to be an example worthy of humanity's imitation. The new birth became a natural change and the promise to do better. Theological modernism viewed Christianity as one more form of natural religion—a mixture of exhortation and experientialism.[29]

THE FUNDAMENTALIST RESPONSE

This radical refashioning of the historic faith drew a reaction from conservative evangelicals who strove to preserve the essential elements of historic Christianity. Evangelical Christianity had its American genesis during the eighteenth century in a movement known as the First Great Awakening. In the American colonies, ministers like George Whitefield, Jonathan Edwards, and Gilbert Tennent worked to revive the churches of the American colonies from the dead, lifeless orthodoxy that had overcome them. Now, in light of this spiritual lethargy, some members of the evangelical community began to stand up for the historical truths embraced by John Wesley, Nicholas von Zinzendorf, and others in Europe, which they believed were essential to the Christian faith: the necessity of a supernatural rebirth; the Bible as God's revelation to humanity; the mandate to spread the gospel; and the death and resurrection of Jesus Christ, which provides a saving relationship with God.[30]

They met in Bible conferences, started Bible institutes, and fought for the control of denominations because they believed that Christianity was at stake. Unlike the modernists, they believed that saving Christianity depended upon maintaining the supernatural elements of the faith that distinguished it from all other religions. They were convinced that to abandon these truths was to abandon the faith itself.

While some recent historians have described this reaction in sociological terms, it is best to understand the fundamentalist movement in its early years as a theological reaction to innovations considered detrimental to the faith delivered "once for all."[31] For example, at the Niagara Bible Conference, begun in 1883, earnest conservatives met to study the Bible in a serious and scientific way. During their annual meetings in Ontario, Canada, near Niagara Falls, the major themes explored each summer included the doctrines of Christ, the Holy Spirit, the Bible, and studies in missions and prophecy.[32] The conference at Niagara eventually produced a statement of essential beliefs, known as the five fundamentals of Niagara. This was subsequently restated later in a variety of forms throughout the years, but the basic formula was orthodox and conservative.

The statement included the doctrine of the physical return of Christ and the participants in the Niagara Bible Conference were generally premillennial. It was agreed that the imminent return of Christ should be omitted because not all conference leaders agreed on that point. Like the church all the way back to the early centuries, the leaders of the conference returned to a confessional expression of the faith.

ORIGINS OF THE FUNDAMENTALIST MOVEMENT

Interdenominational and Conservative

The Niagara Bible Conference established some of the essential foundations of what is today called the fundamentalist movement. It helped to establish the movement as interdenominational and as a result, allowed for a conservative ecumenism. Niagara also provided a platform for world missions, through the ministry of speakers like A. T. Pierson and J. Hudson Taylor, providing the impetus for the faith missions movement. It was also the seedbed for the Bible institute movement. Many of the foot soldiers of the conservative evangelical response to theological modernism were inspired directly or indirectly through the conference and its speakers.[33] The Niagara Conference also gave birth to similar Bible conferences, such as D. L. Moody's efforts at Northfield, Massachusetts.

While the Bible conference movement was solidifying an interdenominational force that focused on the popular study of the Bible and essential doctrines of the faith at the lay level, a group of denominational professors were attempting to concentrate on a scholarly study of the Scriptures and defense of the faith. The most noteworthy group to engage in this pursuit was a core of professors at Princeton Theological Seminary, a Presbyterian school in New Jersey. Since its 1812 beginnings, the school had fought against the encroaching tide of modernism. This group of professors were committed to orthodox Presbyterianism and a key focus of their study was the inspiration of Scripture. Charles Hodge, writing in 1857, argued in favor of plenary inspiration and what he considered the logical corollary doctrine of the inerrancy of the original autographs of the Bible.[34]

Declaring The Fundamentals

The Princeton professors also defended the deity of Christ, His virgin birth, the satisfaction theory of the atonement, and His bodily resurrection. While many argue that these professors did not share all of the values of fundamentalism, Princeton professor B. B. Warfield unquestionably associated himself with the movement through his participation in the publication of a series of booklets aimed at stemming the tide of modernism.

Shortly after the turn of the century, the production of this series of polemic booklets permanently established a movement and a name. Two wealthy oilmen from Los Angeles provided a quarter of a million dollars to supply every Christian worker in the United States with the work, which presented the conservative view of the major theological issues of the day. The work, published initially between 1910 and 1914, consisted of twelve booklets, collectively entitled *The Fundamentals*. A variety of conservative Protestant theologians from the United Kingdom, Canada, and the United States authored essays in the booklets, as they sought to present a case against modernism and for what were now being called the fundamentals of the faith.[35] While broader than the five fundamentals established at the Niagara Conference, the articles offered a conservative response to theological modernism, focusing on higher criticism, the doctrine of the Bible, the Virgin Birth and deity of Christ, substitutionary atonement, and the return of Christ.

The Fundamentals concluded with testimonies from leading conservative Protestants extolling the virtues and life transforming power of the doctrines and ideas presented. The pamphlets, as edited by A. C. Dixon and R. A. Torrey, did not address the creation/evolution debate but did find fault with the Darwinian concept of natural selection.[36] The dispensational model often associated with later developments in fundamentalism was notably absent from the work.[37]

The Fundamentals had two primary effects on the debate over essential Christianity. The editors and benefactors, by calling upon such a wide group of contributors, achieved a broad conservative Protestant consensus. This created an alliance of sorts between seemingly incompatible forces within conservative, evangelical ranks. Those from the Bible institutes, most of whom were interdenominational and generally dispensational (represented by James M. Gray and R. A. Torrey), found themselves cooperating with the seminary-based conservatives who were denominational and predominately nondispensational (represented by B. B. Warfield of Princeton and Y. E. Mullins of Southern Baptist Seminary).[38]

THE FUNDAMENTALIST/MODERNIST CONFLICT

Tolerance Versus Intolerance?

By 1922 the controversy over what was essential to the Christian faith took on a new dimension when Harry Emerson Fosdick, the pastor of Riverside Church in New York City, preached his now famous sermon, "Shall the Fundamentalists Win?" Fosdick strongly suggested that the battle pitted tolerance, as expressed by those who were known as modernists, against intolerance, which he purported to be the core value of the fundamentalists. According to Fosdick, the fundamentalists were harming the Christian church by "quarreling over little matters when the world is dying of great needs."[39] The quarrels referred to were clearly delineated in the body of Fosdick's sermon. Fundamentalists argued for the virgin birth of Jesus Christ, verbal plenary inspiration, the substitutionary death of Christ, and the Second Coming.

Fosdick contended that those who held to such rigid requirements were hopelessly stuck in the past, unable to avail themselves of modern learning. Fosdick argued further that there are two sources of knowledge about God—natural law and the Scriptures.

Many of the early conservatives who supported fundamentalism also embraced this idea. But Fosdick began to apply this principle in a way that undermined Christian doctrine. A secondary effect of Fosdick's sermon was to reinforce the belief that fundamentalists of the late nineteenth century were unlearned and anti-intellectual. Unable to agree with the core beliefs advanced by conservative evangelicals, he labeled them intolerant and ignorant and wrote them off.[40]

Within a year of Fosdick's sermon, a group within the Northern Presbyterian Church produced the Auburn Affirmation, which denied the right of the church to establish theological tests for orthodoxy. The affirmation declared theological positions such as the infallibility of Scripture, the Virgin Birth, the doctrine of substitutionary atonement, the bodily resurrection, and all miracles to be theories about the message of the Bible rather than essential facts upon which an orthodox faith stood.[41]

Machen's Response

That same year, 1923, J. Gresham Machen (the last of the Old Princetonians) took up his pen to produce *Christianity and*

Liberalism. His message was clear: "Despite the liberal use of traditional phraseology modern liberalism not only is a different religion from Christianity but belongs to a totally different class of religions."[42] Through the rest of the book, Machen carefully delineated the essential elements of orthodox Christianity. He affirmed the doctrine of plenary inspiration and inerrancy, the Virgin Birth and deity of Christ, and the doctrine of the substitutionary atonement.[43] A few years later he devoted another entire work to the doctrine of the Virgin Birth. It was important to defend the Virgin Birth because with it stood the authority of the Scriptures.[44] In Machen's mind there was a fundamental difference between conservatives and liberals when it came to Jesus Christ:

> There are generically different views about Jesus, and they are rooted in two generically different views about God and the world. According to one view, God is immanent in the universe in the sense that the universe is the necessary unfolding of His life; and Jesus of Nazareth is a part of that unfolding and supreme product of the same divine forces that are elsewhere operative in the world. According to the other view, God is the Creator of the universe, immanent in it but also eternally separate from it and free; and Jesus of Nazareth came into the universe from outside the universe, to do what nature could never do. The former view is the view of modern naturalism in many different forms; the latter view is the view of the Bible and the Christian Church.[45]

Machen, like the fundamentalists, had identified those crucial core doctrines that had to be defended to save Christianity. If the modernists succeeded in taking the mystery out of the Christian faith and reducing it to a generic ethical system founded by a good moral teacher, all was lost. The supernatural element of Christianity set it apart from the other religions of the world.

Modern science and the new literary criticism were demystifying the faith. If they were successful, they would reduce Christianity to an equal among the world's faiths, no different and certainly not superior or the truth.

Machen already saw this coming to fruition in the Northern Presbyterian Missions Board. In 1932, *Re-thinking Missions* was published. Supported by John D. Rockefeller Jr., the report was cosponsored by a number of Protestant denominations, including the Northern Presbyterians. The report relegated Christianity to one of many religions and urged its readers to avoid any attempts to "destroy" other religions. Instead, it encouraged Christian missionaries to seek ways to support the peaceful coexistence of all of the world's religions. Christianity, it asserted, should not be viewed as distinct from or hostile to other religions around the world.[46]

THE CONFLICT OVER EVOLUTION

By 1925 Darwinism and evolution had become synonymous, and the anti-supernaturalism of Darwinism became the focal point of a popular attempt to stem the tide of modernism and its destruction of the Christian faith. The small Tennessee mining town of Dayton, Tennessee, was the scene for the conclusion of the theological phase of early fundamentalism. Many fundamentalists became concerned about the cultural impact of modernism, particularly through the theory of Darwinian evolution. At the same time, the American Civil Liberties Union (ACLU) watched with growing concern as a number of states enacted laws prohibiting the teaching of evolution in public schools. In 1925 the governor of Tennessee signed into law the Butler Act, which forbade the teaching of evolution in any public school in the state. The goal of the ACLU was to find a high school science teacher in the state of Tennessee who would be willing to test the Butler Act as a violation of the First Amendment guarantee of free speech.

The ACLU advertised widely in order to attract the person they needed to challenge the law. Citizens of the town of Dayton recruited a high school coach to offer himself for the ACLU's test case. The townspeople hoped that this trial would revive the depressed mining town, which had steadily lost population. The subsequent trial took on a life of its own.

By the end of the trial, what had begun as a battle over free speech became a referendum on science and the Bible. An anti-evolution doctrine was not one of the established essentials of the faith within the theological fundamentalist movement.[47] Darwinian evolution, with the idea of natural selection, no intelligent design, and no special divine creation of humans by God, was the issue. This new theme suggested a change in direction for those who felt the need to maintain a strict framework of orthodoxy. No longer fighting on purely theological grounds, the movement began to see itself engaged in a larger sociological conflict vying for the very soul of the American culture.[48] The primary theological focus from 1870 to 1925 gave way to a new central battle. Most see the Scopes Trial in Dayton as the end of fundamentalist respectability and the death of the movement. The excesses and sensational reporting of the events in Dayton pictured fundamentalism to the watching world as old-fashioned and anti-progress.

The fundamentalist movement prior to 1925 was denominationally eclectic, including Presbyterians, Baptists, Methodists, and Reformed Episcopalians. In a very real sense this was a conservative ecumenical movement in which primary theological issues were the focus and secondary theological positions (polity, eschatological nuances, etc.) took a backseat. The list of primary issues was concise. After the Scopes Trial of 1925, fundamentalism began to move beyond a theologically conservative ecumenism toward a more strident conservatism that focused on sociological and cultural concerns. During this period the fundamentalist movement became more militant.[49] Fundamentalists began to dispute about ever more minute issues, preferring to argue among themselves rather than press the essential issues in the broader arena of Christendom. Despite this change in focus, all sides continued to agree that the historic Christian faith had included the key beliefs addressed above since ancient times.

THE FUNDAMENTALS OF THE FAITH

By the end of the nineteenth century, the attempts of conservative evangelicals to stem the effect of liberalizing modernity on the Christian faith had narrowed the list of doctrinal essentials to five key points. The five essentials articulated at the Niagara Bible Conference in 1897 were written specifically because modernism had denied God's supernatural involvement in the writing of the Bible, in human beginnings, and in the salvation of the human race from sin. They were:

- the authority of Scripture,
- the deity of Christ,
- the Virgin Birth,
- substitutionary atonement, and
- the bodily resurrection and physical return of Christ.

This list has been restated in many other contexts since the Niagara Conference. Although some have asserted that the original list was more complete or that a few of the points were different,[50] the five doctrines listed above represent the most common expression of what conservative evangelical Protestants have considered to be the essential elements of the faith. Some might argue that the list could have included a fuller representation of evangelical theology.[51] None, however, can deny the centrality of these five fundamental truths.

These truths continue to be challenged today by those who

propose new doctrines, such as the "openness" of God, as well as by those who question established doctrines like the inerrancy of the Bible, substitutionary atonement, the existence of a literal hell, and the eternal punishment of unbelievers.[52] It is time for the evangelical church to reclaim Christianity's essentials and reaffirm our fundamental doctrines of the faith.

NOTES

1. James I. Packer. *Growing in Christ* (Wheaton: Good News, 1994), 43.
2. Bamber Gascoigne, *The Christians* (New York: William Morrow, 1977), 17.
3. For a thorough treatment of Arius and the doctrine of Arianism, see J. N. D. Kelly, *Early Christian Doctrines* (London: Longmans, Green, 1958), 226–31.
4. *The Creeds of Christendom*, ed. Philip Schaff, vol. 1 (Grand Rapids: Baker, 1983), 27–29.
5. J. N. D. Kelly, *Early Christian Doctrines*, 331–33; see also Louis Berkhof, *The History of Christian Doctrines* (Edinburgh: Banner of Truth Trust, 1937), 107.
6. Schaff, *Creeds of Christendom*, 29. The following appears in the Definition of Chalcedon (p. 451): "Thus have the prophets of old testified; thus the Lord Jesus Christ himself taught us."
7. Anselm, "Why God Became Man," in *Readings in Christian Thought*, ed. Hugh T. Kerr, (Nashville: Abingdon, 1966), 85. As Anselm noted, "Thus, while it is necessary to find a God-Man in whom the integrity of both natures is preserved, it is no less necessary for these two complete natures to meet in one person—just as body and rational soul meet in one man—for otherwise the same person could not be perfect God and perfect man" (pp. 90–91).
8. Ibid., 88.
9. Ibid., 92.
10. Paul Althaus, *The Theology of Martin Luther* (Philadelphia: Fortress, 1966), 202.
11. Ibid., 203.
12. *Creeds of the Churches: A Reader in Christian Doctrine from the Bible to the Present*, ed. John H. Leith (Atlanta: John Knox, 1968), 65.
13. Ibid., 68–69.
14. John Calvin, *The Institutes of the Christian Religion*, trans. Henry Beveridge (2.14, 5) (Grand Rapids, Eerdmans, 1989), 419.
15. Justo Gonzalez, *A History of Christian Thought* (Nashville: Abingdon, 1975), 138–39. See also Calvin, *The Institutes of the Christian Religion* (2.13, 4).
16. Knox returned to his native Scotland in 1559 after years of exile. The following year (1560) the queen regent of Scotland died and left her young daughter, Mary Queen of Scots, to rule alone. With the help of the nobles, Knox established Protestantism as the national religion of Scotland the same year and a new creed (The Scotch Confession of Faith) was formulated. The new queen retaliated against Knox charging him with treason and imprisoning him from 1560 to 1567. He was released after his acquittal by the Scottish Court.
17. *The Creeds of Christendom*, ed. Philip Schaff, vol. 3 (Grand Rapids: Baker, 1983), 446–47.
18. Ibid., 464.

19. "The Westminster Confession of Faith" (chap. 1, sec. 4; chap. 8, sec. 2; and chap. 8, sec. 5), in *Creeds of the Churches*, Leith, ed., 195, 203–4.
20. Gonzalez, *History of Christian Thought*, 238–39. Gonzalez suggested that this is the first clear presentation of the doctrine known as verbal plenary inspiration. Although he suggested that they may have held to a dictation theory, Gonzalez credited these Orthodox Lutherans with maintaining that "the contributions of each writer to the canon show his style, personality, and situation which would suggest a more nuanced theory of inspiration than the dictation theory allows." The place for the writer's style, personality, and situation is critical to the discussion since in the twentieth century, modernists like Harry Emerson Fosdick will accuse fundamentalists of a wooden dictation theory presenting a caricature of a more thoughtful position. See "Shall the Fundamentalists Win?" comp. Michael Warner, *American Sermons: The Pilgrims to Martin Luther King, Jr.* (New York: Library of America, 1999), 780.
21. *The Works of John Wesley* (Grand Rapids: Baker, 1978). See vol. 5, sermons 2, 15, and 20; vol. 6, sermons 42, 62, 70, and 77. In these sermons, among others, Wesley affirms all five of the fundamentals of faith.
22. For a discussion of the various attempts to reconcile faith and science, see Mark Noll, *The Scandal of the Evangelical Mind* (Grand Rapids: Eerdmans, 1994), 177–208; and George Marsden, *Fundamentalism and American Culture* (New York: Oxford, 1980), 118–23.
23. Charles Hodge, "What Is Darwinism?" in *The Princeton Theology 1812–1921: Scripture, Science, and Theological Method from Archibald Alexander to Benjamin Breckinridge Warfield*, ed. Mark A. Noll, 2d ed.(Grand Rapids: Baker, 2001), 149.
24. Ibid., 150. Hodge added (p. 151), "It is the distinctive doctrine of Mr. Darwin that species owe their origin, not to the original intent of the divine mind; not to special acts of creation calling new forms into existence at certain epochs; not to the constant and everywhere operative efficiency of God, guiding physical causes in the production of intended effects; but to the gradual accumulation of unintended variations of structure and instinct, securing some advantage to their subjects."
25. Ibid., 151.
26. Charles A. Briggs, *Higher Criticism of the Hexateuch* (New York: T & T Clark, 1897), 46.
27. Edgar Krentz, *The Historical-Critical Method* (Philadelphia: Fortress, 1975), 30.
28. James I. Packer, *"Fundamentalism" and the Word of God* (Grand Rapids: Eerdmans, 1958), 37.
29. Ibid., 27.
30. Noll, *Scandal of the Evangelical Mind*, 9.
31. David Beale, *In Pursuit of Purity: American Fundamentalism Since 1850* (Greenville, S.C.: Bob Jones Univ., 1986), 29. Beale indicated that the political and sociological issues that become a distinct part of the fundamentalist movement in the 1920 and beyond was not present at Niagara. "Naturally there were distinct differences between old Niagara's embryonic Fundamentalism and the movement since the 1920s. For instance, although the Niagara leaders expressed interest in political conservatism and patriotism, they rarely mentioned these things."
32. Ibid., 27. Beale indicated that while premillennialism dominated the conferences, speakers expressed both pretribulational and posttribulational rapture positions.
33. Ibid., 29–31.

34. Hodge, "Inspiration," *Princeton Theology*, 137. "An inspired man could not err in his instruction on any subject."

35. Sydney Ahlstrom, *A Religious History of the American People* (New Haven, Conn.: Yale Univ. Press, 1972), 815.

36. R. A. Torrey and A. C. Dixon, eds., *The Fundamentals: A Testimony to the Truth* (Chicago: n.p., n.d.). In volume 4, chapter 4, James Orr of Glasgow, Scotland, discussed "Science and the Christian Faith." In his writing he argued that evolution and the creation account of Genesis need not be viewed as incompatible." He wrote: "The conclusion of the whole is, that, up to the present hour, science and the Biblical views of God, man, and the world, do not stand in any real relation of conflict" (104). In volume 7, chapter 1, George Frederick Wright of Oberlin College argues that the real issue is not so much evolution as Darwinism, which "practically eliminates God from the whole creative process." He concludes his thoughts by writing, "The evidence for evolution, even in its milder form, does not begin to be as strong as that for the revelation of God in the Bible" (20).

37. George W. Dollar, *A History of Fundamentalism* (Greenville, S.C.: Bob Jones Univ, 1973), 175–76.

38. Ahlstrom, *A Religious History*, 815–16. At least during the period between 1870 and 1925, conservatives attempting to stem the tide of modernism were much broader and more focused on what they perceived to be the essential elements of the Christian faith. While there were those within the movement who could be viewed as militant, the movement was still primarily defensive rather than offensive.

39. Harry Emerson Fosdick, "Shall the Fundamentalists Win?" comp. Michael Warner, *American Sermons: The Pilgrims to Martin Luther King, Jr.* (New York: Library of America Press, 1999), 785.

40. Ibid., 783–85.

41. D. G. Hart and John Muether, *Fighting the Good Fight: A Brief History of the Orthodox Presbyterian Church* (Philadelphia: Committee for the Historian of the Orthodox Presbyterian Church, 1995), 24.

42. J. Gresham Machen, *Christianity and Liberalism* (Grand Rapids: Eerdmans, 1946), 7.

43. Ibid., 74, 114, 117.

44. J. Gresham Machen, *The Virgin Birth of Christ* (New York: Harper & Row, 1930), 382.

45. Ibid., 387.

46. Hart and Muether, *Fighting the Good Fight*, 27.

47. Dollar, *A History of Fundamentalism*, 72–73.

48. Marsden, *Fundamentalism and American Culture*, 185. For a history of the movement from the 1930s through the middle of the twentieth century, see Joel Carpenter, *Revive Us Again: The Reawakening of American Fundamentalism* (New York: Oxford Univ. Press, 1997).

49. Ibid., 1. "A more precise statement of the same point is that an American fundamentalist is an evangelical who is in militant opposition to liberal theology in the churches or to changes in cultural values or mores, such as those associated with 'secular humanism.'" While Marsden attempts to apply that term to the entire history of Christian fundamentalism in America, it appears better to use this as the post-1925 definition. Theological fundamentalism (1870–1925) was far more concerned with consolidating and maintaining the faithful and arguing on theological grounds rather than cultural and sociological grounds.

50. Dollar, *A History of Fundamentalism*, 72–73. Dollar lists the original five points as "the inspiration of the Bible, the depravity of man, redemption through Christ's

blood, the true church made up of all believers, and the coming of the Lord to set up His reign" (72). He also argues that the "original list of fundamentals included the Trinity, the fall of Adam, the need of the new birth, full deliverance of guilt at salvation, the assurance of salvation, the centrality of Christ in the Bible, the walk after the Spirit, the resurrection of both believers and unbelievers, and the ripening of the present age for judgment" (73).

51. Richard J. Mouw, *The Smell of Sawdust* (San Francisco: HarperCollins, 2000), 71–72. Mouw argues that the list of the fundamentals does not represent the whole of the conservative evangelical theology. Yet as we know from the history of the movement, it has presented itself as theologically shallow at times.

52. Timothy Morgan, "Theologians Decry 'Narrow' Boundaries," *Christianity Today*, 10 June 2002, 18.

———

Thomas Cornman is dean of the undergraduate school at the Moody Bible Institute. He holds the Ph.D. degree in U.S. history from the University of Illinois, Chicago, as well as degrees from Philadelphia College of the Bible, Talbot School of Theology, and Temple University.

2

BUILT UPON THE TRUTH

BIBLICAL AUTHORITY YESTERDAY AND TODAY

David Finkbeiner

Millard Erickson has defined *authority* as "the right to command belief and/or action."[1] Christians rightly recognize that there is no higher authority than God. His right to command belief and action is unique. After all, God is Creator and therefore has the right of ownership over everything (cf. Ps. 24:1; Rom. 9:19–21), His omnipotence gives Him the sovereign power to support His right of ownership (cf. Job 42:2; Jeremiah 32:17), and His unlimited knowledge and wisdom render His judgments unquestionable (cf. Rom. 11:33–36; Job 38:1–42:62). Indeed, all authority derives from Him (cf. Rom. 13:1).

This is why discussions of biblical authority are never far removed from the question of the Bible's divine status. In what sense can it be considered *God's* Word? Theologians have tended to answer this question in one of two ways: Scripture is God's Word either because of what it is or because of what it does.[2] The latter view maintains that Scripture *functions* authoritatively in the church because the Holy Spirit uses it in some way in believers' lives. The former view maintains that the Spirit uses Scripture precisely because of what it *is:* the very Word of God. This view, therefore, emphasizes the doctrine of inspiration. It has been the traditional view of the church throughout history, though it came under attack in the modern era with the rise of higher criticism.

BIBLICAL AUTHORITY AND HIGHER CRITICISM

When applied to the study of the Bible, *criticism* itself is not necessarily a dirty word. For example, all conservative evangelical scholars consider *textual criticism* (also called *lower criticism*) to be a crucial discipline. This is because it seeks to determine from among variant manuscripts the original reading of any given Old Testament or New Testament text, a vital task to anyone who takes the words of Scripture seriously.[3] In addition, *biblical criticism* may be defined as nothing more than a deliberate, careful study of the biblical text to "see Scripture exactly as it is," an endeavor all evangelicals would consider appropriate.[4]

Higher criticism, however, is an entirely different matter because, as generally understood, it is tied to the "historical-critical method." While even conservative scholars readily recognize that proper interpretation of a biblical text demands an understanding of its historical background (because the biblical text was written in a particular historical context), higher criticism and the historical-critical method go much further than that. At its heart, higher criticism is committed to "historical consciousness." This means that the biblical texts must be understood merely as a product of their own human culture and history.[5] Higher critics see Scripture as temporally and culturally bound rather than eternally significant, as error-prone rather than in-errant, as natural rather than supernatural. Consequently, they believe that the Bible should be studied like any other human book. It has no privileged position when analyzed by the critical scholar, and its inspiration should be ignored. In short, higher criticism emphasizes the humanity of Scripture to the exclusion of its divine side.

Higher criticism had great impact in the United States late in the nineteenth century, but its origins in Europe were much earlier.[6] Higher criticism began to take clear shape in the mid-seventeenth century, particularly among British and French thinkers. By the mid-eighteenth century it had established a foothold in Germany, where it flourished and continued to grow in influence along with the rising prestige of the German university in the nineteenth century.[7] Granted, the United States had its share of negative biblical critics in the eighteenth and early nineteenth centuries (e.g., Thomas Paine, Thomas Jefferson, Unitarians), but higher criticism itself did not really begin seriously to influence the American religious world until after the Civil War. Between the 1870s and the 1930s, belief in the Bible as the infallible Word of God eroded considerably.

Higher criticism's march to dominance began with early skirmishes with conservatives in the 1880s[8] and moved on to more pitched battles with denominations and institutions in the 1890s. Despite some early setbacks in those battles, higher criticism's influence grew so that by 1910–1915 it was a major focus of concern for the writers of *The Fundamentals*.[9] By the 1920s, opponents of higher criticism would be forced from their denominations (e.g., J. Gresham Machen's forced exit from the Northern Presbyterian denomination).[10]

Early on, one can generally distinguish at least three responses to higher criticism: liberal, moderate, and conservative.[11] Liberals not only advocated the use of higher criticism, they also embraced its most skeptical and anti-supernatural conclusions.

Hence, they did not attempt to make higher criticism compatible with orthodox Christian theology. Moderates, on the other hand, did have such a concern. They strongly supported the use of higher criticism, and they were very willing to accept minor errors in Scripture. However, they were believing scholars who held to orthodox Christian beliefs and had no intention of abandoning them. Indeed, they were convinced that orthodoxy was compatible with and, in fact, well served by higher criticism.

Conservatives were not so convinced. They rejected the results of higher criticism because its results undermined traditional understandings of Scripture (e.g., the Mosaic authorship of the Pentateuch) and freely recognized the presence of error in the biblical text. They were troubled by the fact that higher criticism, in its zeal to embrace the humanity of Scripture, undermined its divinity. For them, higher criticism denied Scripture's infallibility and, in so doing, also denied its inspiration and authority.

These conservative evangelicals of the late nineteenth and early twentieth centuries—many of whom we have called "paleo-fundamentalists"—chose to fight against the inroads of the historical-critical method and to defend the inspiration of Scripture. Though there were many advocates of the traditional view, the true champions of the cause were the theologians who came out of old Princeton Seminary, particularly Benjamin Breckinridge Warfield. Warfield and his colleagues represent the most articulate expression of the view held by the paleo-fundamentalists. What did they teach about biblical authority?

BIBLICAL AUTHORITY YESTERDAY: INSPIRATION

It is important to understand at the outset that the Princetonian view of biblical authority was not simply their own invention. They saw themselves as recapitulating and refining the central tradition of the church on biblical authority at a time when that tradition was under attack. Contrary to the claims of some, the Princetonian view of biblical authority was not an innovation.[12] Woodbridge wrote:

> Is biblical inerrancy a fundamentalist doctrine? If this question means, Do fundamentalists uphold biblical inerrancy? the answer is obviously yes. If the question means, Do fundamentalists alone uphold the doctrine? then the answer is no. Biblical inerrancy properly defined is a fundamental doctrine that many evangelicals throughout the centuries have upheld. . . . Evangelicals remain squarely in the so-called central tradition of the Christian churches when they affirm that the Bible is infallible not only for matters of faith and practice but also for its discussions of history and the natural world.[13]

This means that we have good reason to explore the Princetonians' doctrine of biblical authority, because in doing so, we really are seeing a careful restatement of the central tradition of the church, a tradition rooted in the teaching of the Bible itself.

At the heart of the Princetonians' statement of biblical authority is their doctrine of inspiration. The Princetonian definition of inspiration can be summarized in the following statement: *Inspiration is that supernatural work of the Holy Spirit by which He superintended the writing process of Scripture so that all the words and every part of the original writings were at the same time the words of the human writers and the very words of God.* This definition contains four key elements.

1. Inspiration is a supernatural superintendence by the Spirit.

In contrast to the higher critic's commitment to naturalism, paleo-fundamentalists embraced the idea that God could act supernaturally in this world. If not, then miracles like Israel's exodus from Egypt, Jesus' virgin birth, and His resurrection were not possible. Hence, they also emphasized the idea that inspiration should be understood in supernatural rather than natural terms. For them, inspiration was far more than some quaint way to describe particularly insightful human writings (as, for example, when we say that Shakespeare's works are "inspired," in the sense of being outstandingly artistic and insightful) or some special heightening of human powers by the Holy Spirit. It was a direct act of God the Holy Spirit in the very writing of Scripture.

Commitment to inspiration as a supernatural work does not deny God's providential preparation of the human authors to write Scripture, a preparation whose means are admittedly more "natural" than "supernatural."[14] Indeed, for the Princetonians God's sovereign preparation of the human writers was a crucial companion to the work of inspiration.[15] What it does deny is that inspiration is to be identified with this sovereign preparation. God providentially prepared these writers to write just what they did, but He did not just leave them to their own devices when it came time to write. The Spirit was also supernaturally involved in the very writing process itself.

Hence, the Spirit's supernatural work of inspiration is described as "superintendence." While the term could be understood in a more indirect sense as a sort of passive overseeing or oblique influence, the Princetonians meant it in a more immediate, active sense.[16] God the Holy Spirit was directly at work in the very writing of Scripture so that, while human, the words of Scripture are also fully divine. Providential guidance could only produce the writings of godly men, but the Holy Spirit's superintendence was needed to produce a text that is divine. So Warfield wrote that, in His work of superintending inspiration,

the Spirit of God, flowing confluently in with the providentially and graciously determined work of men, spontaneously producing under the Divine directions the writings appointed to them, gives the product a Divine quality unattainable by human powers alone. Thus these books become not merely the word of godly men, but the immediate word of God Himself, speaking directly as such to the minds and hearts of every reader.[17]

The term *inspiration* has a long pedigree as the name for this superintending process, and it has often been used to translate *theopneustos*, the biblical term describing this activity in 2 Timothy 3:16. The Princetonians, however, pointed out that *theopneustos* is better translated as "God-breathed." They were concerned that the English term "inspiration" could be misunderstood because its imagery suggests breathing into, as if God either breathes into the human writers before they write the Scriptures, or breathes into the already written Scriptures to make them spiritually powerful. But *theopneustos* conveys neither of those ideas. It means that all the Scriptures are God's words, breathed out by Him. Warfield summarized this point: "What is declared by this fundamental passage is simply that the Scriptures are a divine product, without any indication of how God has operated in producing them."[18] Second Peter 1:20–21 gives us more insight into this process. In talking about Scripture, it declares that Scripture's origins are not by the will of man. Instead, while the human authors of Scripture did speak, these men "spoke from God as they were carried along [from the Greek *pheromenoi*] by the Holy Spirit." Warfield translated the term *pheromenoi* as "borne" and pointed out the significance of the term:

> The term here used is not to be confounded with guiding, or directing, or controlling, or even leading in the full sense of that word. It goes beyond all such terms, in assigning the effect produced specifically to the active agent. What is "borne" is taken up by the "bearer" and conveyed by the "bearer's" power, not its own, to the "bearer's" goal, not its own. The men who spoke from God are here declared, therefore, to

have been taken up by the Holy Spirit and brought by His power to the goal of His choosing.[19]

In short, then, inspiration is a divine activity that results in a divine product, as 2 Timothy 3:16 and 2 Peter 1:20–21 testify.

2. Inspiration pertains to the original writings.

The Princetonians were careful to maintain that this divine written product, described in 2 Timothy 3:16 as God-breathed, is to be identified explicitly with what the human authors of Scripture originally wrote—what are often called the *autographs*. This means that Hebrew and Greek copies of those autographs and translations of Scripture into other languages are inspired only to the extent that they accurately reflect the originals. Inspiration does not pertain to the copying or translation process.

In his article "The Inerrancy of the Original Autographs," Warfield made several important clarifications about the inspiration of the autographs. First, while it is true that we no longer have the autographs themselves, it is a gross exaggeration to claim that the original words of Scripture have disappeared. We do have access to those original words in the extant copies of those autographs (which is why textual criticism and careful translation are so crucial). Just because God did not inspire the copyists does not mean He has not acted providentially to preserve the text. Second, maintaining the inspiration of the autographs is important because it distinguishes inspired Scripture from the errors introduced into the text by careless copyists, mistaken translators, and inattentive printers. Of course, the recognition of such copying and translation errors is not a cure-all to explain away all of the difficulties critics raise against the text of Scripture. Even with a completely accurate copy of the autographs, faithful believers would still need to diligently study and defend the veracity of the biblical text. Third, the inspiration of the autographs is nothing new; believers throughout church history have valued the importance of an accurately preserved text and careful translation because they believed in the inspiration of the autographs.[20]

3. *Inspiration is verbal and plenary.*

This view of inspiration often has been described as *verbal* and *plenary*. Both terms were crucial to the Princetonian understanding of inspiration. Plenary inspiration means that *all* the Bible, Scripture in its entirety, is *fully* inspired by God. Hence, against those who would say that only certain parts of Scripture (for example, its doctrine or its ethics) are inspired while other parts (for example, its statements pertaining to history or science) are not, plenary inspiration declares that every part of Scripture is inspired. In addition, against those who would argue that there are different degrees of inspiration in Scripture (for instance, doctrinal statements are more inspired than historical statements), plenary inspiration maintains that all of Scripture is equally inspired. Furthermore, against those who hold that only those parts of Scripture that God uses to subjectively speak to the individual are inspired, plenary inspiration insists that the whole of Scripture is God's Word.

The Princetonians rightly maintained that 2 Timothy 3:16 clearly teaches plenary inspiration in its assertion that "all Scripture is God-breathed."[21] Scripture does not merely *contain* the Word of God; it *is* the Word of God.

Verbal inspiration means that inspiration extends to the very words of Scripture. Consequently, against those who would maintain that inspiration consists in God's mere providential preparation of the human writers, verbal inspiration insists that God is involved in the writing of the very words themselves. And against those who say that God inspires only the thoughts of the human writers, verbal inspiration insists that God-inspired thoughts cannot be separated from God-inspired words.[22]

Here too the Princetonians rightly maintained that verbal inspiration was the view taught in Scripture itself. Warfield cited several New Testament passages which, in making arguments from Old Testament passages viewed as God's Word, base their arguments on a single word in that passage: Matthew 22:32 (a present tense verb); Matthew 22:43–45 (a word); John 10:34–35 (a word); Galatians 3:16 (a singular noun).[23] Hodge and Warfield cited 1 Corinthians 2:13 as an example of verbal inspiration, where "Paul claims that the Holy Spirit guaranteed his words as well as his thoughts."[24]

According to the Princetonians, it is very important to recognize that verbal inspiration does not necessarily demand a particular mode of inspiration. That is, verbal inspiration should not necessarily be confused with a certain theory of inspiration known as the "dictation" or "mechanical" theory of inspiration. In this theory, the human writers are little more than pens, taking down word for word what God dictates to them to write. It is true that some advocates of verbal inspiration throughout history (including some paleo-fundamentalists) have spoken this way, though it is also likely that in most cases they were simply trying to emphasize that the Bible is God's Word.[25] But in its best expression, early fundamentalism (and certainly the Princetonians!) rejected a dictation model.[26] While recognizing that certain parts of Scripture may have been dictated (e.g., the Ten Commandments), the Princetonians found dictation wanting as a general theory of inspiration precisely because it did not take the humanity of Scripture as seriously as Scripture itself does.

4. Inspiration involves divine and human authorship (concursis).

The Princetonians insisted that verbal-plenary inspiration meant that Scripture is at one and the same time both the very words of God and the words of the human authors. This dual authorship has been called "concursis" or "confluence." In his article "The Divine and Human in the Bible," Warfield explained that both the divine and human must be given their due. It is incorrect to emphasize the divine to the exclusion of the human (as in dictation models), or to emphasize the human to the exclusion of the divine (as in higher criticism), or to think that they are incompatible such that certain portions of Scripture are divine while the rest are merely human.[27] So Warfield wrote:

> The human and divine factors in inspiration are conceived of as flowing confluently and harmoniously to the production of a common product. And the two elements are conceived of in the Scriptures as the inseparable constituents of one single and uncompounded product. Of every word of Scripture is it to be affirmed, in turn, that it is God's word and that it is man's word. All the qualities of divinity and of humanity are to be sought and may be found in every portion and element of the Scripture; while, on the other hand, no quality inconsistent with either divinity or humanity can be found in any portion or element of Scripture.[28]

Warfield pointed out that Scripture itself testifies to its own humanity and divinity. On the human side, besides clear differences between writers in terms of style and vocabulary and explicit claims to human authorship (for example, Paul's letters), several portions of Scripture are ascribed to their human writers (e.g., Matt. 22:24; Mark 7:6, 10; Rom. 10:19, 20; 11:9). Furthermore, there are several passages which indicate, consistent with 2 Peter 1:20–21, that the human authors spoke by the Holy Spirit —or He spoke through them (Mark 12:36; Acts 1:16; 4:25). In fact, God's words and the human author's words are so closely identified that in certain places words clearly ascribed to God in the Old Testament are ascribed to the human author in the New Testament (cf. Ex. 20:12; 21:17 with Mark 7:10).[29]

On the divine side, we have already seen the teaching of central passages like 2 Timothy 3:16–17 and 2 Peter 1:20–21, which clearly assert that Scripture is inspired and should be regarded as God's very Word. Warfield found much biblical support to establish that Scripture teaches clearly that it is God's Word. For example, there are passages that indicate that what Scripture says, God says (cf. Gen. 2:24 with Matt. 19:4–5); and conversely, what God says, Scripture says (cf. Ex. 9:16 with Rom. 9:17). In addition, Jesus' own view of Scripture attests to its being God's Word.[30]

BIBLICAL AUTHORITY TODAY: IMPLICATIONS OF INSPIRATION

In essence, then, inspiration maintains that the words of Scripture, while being certainly the words of the human authors, are also the words of God. This is precisely why for the Princetonians Scriptural authority cannot be separated from its inspiration. Scripture has such unmitigated authority because it is God's very own Word, bearing His own authority. The nature of Scripture so described has at least four implications.

1. God's Word is supremely authoritative.

Because it is God's Word, Scripture bears the highest authority possible: that of God Himself. This is precisely why the Princetonians were unequivocally committed to the Reformation doctrine of *sola scriptura*. This doctrine means that Scripture alone is our only final authority because Scripture, due to its inspiration, uniquely preserves God's revelation to humanity.

Early Princetonians like Archibald Alexander emphasized Scripture's final authority contrary to the Roman Catholic view, which acknowledged the equal legitimacy of church tradition along with Scripture. This focus reiterated the Protestant theme that even the traditions and teachings of the church must be subject to the final authority of divine Scripture. But beginning with Charles Hodge, other foils of *sola scriptura* emerged in the Princetonian discussion of biblical authority: mysticism and rationalism.[31]

Mysticism has various forms, but at its core it subordinates Scripture to the subjective experience of the human being. Warfield described it this way:

> Its characteristic conception is that the Christian man has something within himself,—call it enlightened reason, spiritual insight, the Christian consciousness, the witness of the Spirit, or call it what you will,—to the test of which every "external revelation" is to be subjected, and according to the decision of which are the contents of the Bible to be valued.[32]

For example, if a person claims that only those parts of the Bible that God uses to speak to her are truly God's Word, she is taking a mystical view. Such a view undercuts *sola scriptura* because a person's subjective experience is the final authority, not the text of Scripture. The Princetonians did not deny that the Holy Spirit does indeed use Scripture to speak to us, but they insisted that He speaks to us today by means of what He has already spoken in the very words of Scripture themselves.

Rationalism also undercuts *sola scriptura*. Like mysticism, it too has many forms. But at its heart it subjects Scripture to human rationality in its attempt to distinguish between its inspired and its uninspired elements.[33] For paleo-fundamentalists, it constituted the single greatest threat to the final divine authority of Scripture in the form of higher criticism. Higher critics who denied the full inspiration of the Bible—or its inspiration at all—were in effect placing the judgments of human reason above the authority of Scripture itself. In sum, the Princetonians maintained that if the Bible is inspired in the way described above, it must be the final authority over human tradition, experience, and reason.

2. God's Word is inerrant.

Because the Bible is *God's* Word, the Princetonians rightly maintained that it is also inerrant—without error in what it affirms.[34] Paul Feinberg's contemporary definition of inerrancy captures more precisely what the Princetonians meant by the term: "When all the facts become known, they will demonstrate that the Bible in its original autographs and correctly interpreted is entirely true and never false in all it affirms, whether that relates to doctrine or ethics or to the social, physical, or life sciences."[35]

For the Princetonians, Scripture's inerrancy was inseparable from its inspiration and authority. Thus Warfield wrote that verbal-plenary inspiration "preserves its product from everything inconsistent with a divine authorship—thus securing, among other things, that entire truthfulness which is everywhere presupposed in and asserted for Scripture by the Biblical writers (inerrancy)."[36] This does not mean, of course, that we should think of Scripture as a science or history textbook. Scripture does not purport to be an encyclopedia of all such knowledge, nor does it speak of all this knowledge in technical, precise language. But whenever Scripture does address any matter, what it affirms in the ordinary language of the human author does not err.[37]

Hodge and Warfield pointed out that the consequences of an error would be devastating: "It is plain, however, that if the Scriptures do fail in truth in their statements of whatever kind, the doctrine of inspiration which has been defended in this paper [i.e., verbal-plenary inspiration] cannot stand."[38] Why? Because God, who is trustworthy, faithful, and true (e.g., Deut. 7:9; Rev. 19:11), who never lies (1 Sam. 15:29; Titus 1:2), and who knows all things (Job 37:16; 1 John 3:20), would then be either mistaken or deceptive, and either is unthinkable. Hence, in Scripture God Himself declares that His words are true, pure, trustworthy, and without error (Ps. 12:6; 119:160).

In the end, inerrancy comes down to a question of authority. When God makes a statement in Scripture, will we believe it, or will we believe a human standard by which critics claim it to be in error?[39] Jesus Himself answered this question when He said, "Scripture cannot be broken" (John 10:34–35). Warfield explained Jesus' words this way: "It is impossible for the Scripture to be annulled, its authority to be withstood, or denied"; its authority is irrefutable because it bears God's authority.[40]

Despite the Princetonians' sound biblical and theological reasoning on this point, critics were not convinced. Unbelieving critics (who were very liberal theologically) simply rejected their arguments because they did not take inspiration seriously—just like they did not take many orthodox doctrines seriously. Believing critics who did take inspiration seriously but refused to acknowledge inerrancy could not be so dismissive of the Princetonian arguments. They generally adopted two strategies to respond to the Princetonian case for inerrancy.

Their first strategy was to reject verbal-plenary inspiration and simply redefine the term so that it does not entail inerrancy. Some of these opponents of verbal-plenary inspiration—most notably Charles Briggs—actually denied that verbal-plenary inspiration and inerrancy were the central tradition of the church. Briggs argued that many theological luminaries throughout church history believed that the Bible is infallible in religious matters, even though it might contain incidental errors in history or science. The Princetonian response was a compelling demonstration that the church's central tradition has always been consistent with verbal-plenary inspiration and inerrancy in the autographs.[41]

Others acknowledged that verbal-plenary inspiration was the traditional view of the church but argued that alleged discrepancies and certain undeniable "facts" uncovered by higher criticism made belief in the traditional view no longer tenable.[42] The Princeton theologians countered that the method of developing a doctrine of Scripture must indeed be inductive, but its important data are not the phenomena. Our doctrine of Scripture must be based on what Scripture itself *teaches* about its own inspiration; then we interpret alleged discrepancies accordingly.

Some believing critics also adopted a second strategy to respond to the Princetonian arguments for inerrancy. They argued for a certain understanding of God's "accommodation" to humanity. It is widely recognized that "God accommodated Himself to our human weakness and limited capacity to understand His thoughts by communicating to us through human words."[43] After all, God is infinite and human beings are finite. But these critics took this idea further. They argued that to communicate to us, God had to accommodate Himself, not just to limited human language, but also to the false ideas and thought forms of a given human culture. The difference is huge, as Warfield explained: "It is one thing to adapt the teaching of truth to the stage of receptivity of the learner; it is another thing to adopt the errors of the time as the very matter to be taught."[44] Not only does such an approach undercut Scripture's clear testimony to its plenary inspiration, it also makes God deceptive and incapable of communicating truthfully to human beings.[45] But our all-powerful and wise God can communicate to us in human words that, because they are at the same time His own words, do not err.

3. God's Word communicates truth.

As God's *Word*, Scripture communicates truth. This fact involves three points. First, the Princetonians were convinced that God's Word *communicates*. This belief stemmed from the Reformation conviction regarding the perspicuity of Scripture—the idea that Scripture's basic meaning is clear so that we do not need a divine interpreter to give us its message. Warfield pointed out that the impact of higher criticism was devastating to the clarity of Scripture, because now God's Word had to be sifted and evaluated by a scholarly elite who could tell laypeople what could be believed. This represented a loss not merely of the Protestant doctrine of the perspicuity of the Scriptures, but with it of all that that doctrine is meant to express and safeguard—the loss of the Bible itself to the very plain Christian man for all practical purposes, and the delivery of his conscience over to the tender mercies of his human instructors, whether ecclesiastical or scholastic.[46]

Warfield was not alone in such sentiments. Timothy Weber points out that fundamentalists in general consistently believed that, instead of "taking the Bible away from the Church" as the critics had done, they were keeping "the Bible in the hands of common believers." Therefore, in combating higher criticism, they "believed that they had saved the Bible for the church."[47] This was not to deny the need for teachers and scholars; it simply made it possible for laypeople to follow the noble example of the ancient Bereans, who "examined the Scriptures every day to see if what Paul said was true" (Acts 17:11).

The perspicuity of Scripture guarantees that its meaning is accessible. The Princetonians and paleo-fundamentalists were highly confident that, even though interpretive disagreements clearly existed, those who humbly and diligently studied the text could discover the true meaning of the text. Meaning should be inductively taken out of the text, not deductively read into the text. So confident were they of the accessibility of meaning, in fact, that they have often been criticized for a certain naiveté in not taking seriously enough the effect that presuppositions have on the interpretive process—a naiveté shared by much of their culture, we might add. But even if objective interpretation is harder to come by than they might have thought, their emphasis on accessible meaning was an important one.

Second, the Princeton theologians assumed that God's Word communicates *truth*. By "truth" we mean doctrine, teaching, or information about God and the world that accurately describes the way things are.[48] This does not mean, of course, that the

Princetonians believed that the Bible does nothing other than affirm such information; it certainly does more than that. Nevertheless, they emphasized that Scripture does communicate true information, an emphasis that becomes more controversial in our day.[49]

Third, the fact that God communicates truth to human beings in human language means that the faithful student of Scripture must make use of historical-grammatical interpretation. This approach seeks to understand what the human author tried to communicate to his audience in his day, and so it demands careful attention to the text's original language, historical background, and other textual details. As Hodge and Warfield put it, "Exegesis must be historical as well as grammatical, and must always seek the meaning *intended,* not any meaning that can be tortured out of a passage."[50] The conviction here is that God speaks to us today by what He spoke through the human author when the biblical text was written. In order to understand what God says to us, we must understand what He said through the human author in his context.[51]

4. God's Word communicates to us.

As God's *Word,* the inspired Bible is used by God to speak to us today. Warfield wrote that when the believer reads the Word, he "can listen directly to the Divine voice itself speaking immediately in the Scriptural word to him." He appealed to passages like Romans 15:4 and 1 Corinthians 10:11 to show that Scripture pertains to all redemptive history, to present and future redemptive history as well as the past, so that God's Word in Scripture is preserved for all His people at all times.[52]

The Princetonians believed that Scripture has a life-shaping impact on His church; it is "a work of the Spirit for spiritual ends."[53] Warfield pointed out that Scripture makes us, in Paul's words, wise unto salvation. In fact, Scripture itself is part of God's work of redemption.[54] When we recognize concursive Scripture for what it is, we do "full justice . . . to human needs" because Scripture really does touch human beings at their heart, impacting them in numerous ways to change them.[55] Hence, Scripture does not just give us facts to know; it shapes our very lives. Put differently, the Spirit works in inspiration to give us His very Word, and He continues to work in illumination to bring that Word to bear in our lives. In this sense, then, the Princetonians were consistent with the Reformation understanding of Word and Spirit: the Spirit gives us His Word and continues to endow it with His life-giving power today.

BIBLICAL AUTHORITY TODAY: INSPIRATION AND ITS IMPLICATIONS

The story of a conservative view of biblical authority did not end in the 1920s when the modernists won control of the mainline denominations. Though higher criticism is still extremely influential, full biblical authority is alive and well in conservative evangelicalism today, as are many of the debates accompanying it. As the old Princeton theology articulated and shaped the fundamentalist view of inspiration, so too it has continued to shape conservative evangelicalism. Writing about a century after Hodge and Warfield's famous "Inspiration" article, Roger Nicole could say that "after almost one hundred years this article in its main positions has hardly aged,"[56] and little has changed since Nicole wrote those words. Even if they continue to restate and refine it, conservative evangelicals still firmly embrace concursive verbal-plenary inspiration because, like the Princetonians, they believe that it represents the teaching of Scripture itself and the central tradition of the church.[57]

What difference does this traditional understanding of inspiration make for us today? As with inspiration itself, the four implications of inspiration are still widely embraced among evangelicals today. Many of them have been vigorously attacked in ways different from the days of the paleo-fundamentalists. But all of them continue to be refined and defended in light of contemporary debates.

1. God's Word is still supremely authoritative.

Today evangelicals continue to remain committed to the doctrine of *sola scriptura* (the Bible is our only final authority). But this commitment does not go unchallenged. As in Warfield's day, rationalistic and mystical forces continue to confront biblical authority. Higher criticism, entrenched as it is in many academic circles, still challenges the claims of Scripture—sometimes in ways far more radical than in Warfield's day.[58]

In our own day, however, mysticism may be an even greater challenge to Scripture's final authority. Many people in our culture often speak glibly about spirituality, but it is a spirituality of their own making. For them, the Bible has no claim over their lives unless they choose to grant it that right. Furthermore, they do not necessarily consider the Bible to be unique, nor do they believe that it has *universal* authority. Indeed, any claim that the Bible is God's revelation for all humanity is considered bigoted. It is only authoritative to those who choose to accept its worldview, since many other worldviews are equally legitimate.

Even believers in good evangelical churches can be influenced by mysticism when they are tempted to choose those teachings of Scripture that they find attractive or useful to them while ignoring other relevant passages. For example, it is tempting to focus on passages that emphasize God's love and kindness toward people —because this is comforting to us and winsome to our culture— while virtually ignoring passages that speak of God's wrath, often in graphic, horrifying imagery (e.g., Rev. 19:11–21, especially 15, 21).[59]

Beyond mysticism and rationalism, other forces also challenge *sola scriptura* today. Roman Catholicism and Eastern Orthodoxy continue to confront the evangelical commitment to Scripture as the only final authority for Christians. In addition, some theologians think of the Bible less as an authority and more as a resource or tool used in various ways by God and His people to shape the Christian community, giving the Scriptures only a "functional authority." While that may be true as far as it goes, it is also necessary to stress that the Bible is an effective resource for shaping believers *because* it is God's authoritative Word.

Most pernicious of all, some theologians today reject the very notion of religious authority at all. This is consistent, for example, with contemporary theological movements like process theology (where God Himself is seen not as an authority but as a fellow participant with human beings in creating the ongoing world) and feminist theology (where the ideas of authority and hierarchy are seen as inherently male and anti-female). Indeed, the very idea of authority is not particularly popular in our culture in general. But if the God of the Bible exists, He has undisputed authority. And if He has spoken in His Word, it bears His undisputed and final authority yesterday, today, and tomorrow.

2. God's Word is still inerrant.

Like the fundamentalist movement before it, the evangelical movement that emerged in the 1940s also was thoroughly committed to inerrancy, at least initially. However, while a great many evangelicals still subscribe to inerrancy, since the 1960s a certain segment of evangelicalism has abandoned the doctrine, at least in substance.[60] The debate that has ensued is remarkably similar to the debate between the Princetonians and believing critics led by Charles Briggs. Indeed, for us it creates, in the words of Mark Noll, "a sense of déjà vu upon reading Warfield's various writings on the nature of biblical authority."[61] Several questions have emerged in this debate.

First, what alternatives have evangelicals who have rejected inerrancy proposed? Many of them have, as in Warfield's day, argued that Scripture's accuracy only pertains to its religiously important content—matters of faith and practice or God's saving purpose—rather than in every area Scripture addresses. In these other areas "incidental" errors may have crept in due to God's "accommodation." Others have asserted that inerrancy is a relatively trivial doctrine. They maintain that defenders of inerrancy get so caught up in polemic debates and arguments over minutia that they fail to focus on the major issues of the faith and unduly cause division.[62] Others maintain that inerrantists misunderstand the purpose of the Bible. The Bible, they argue, is concerned first and foremost with shaping Christian lives, not making accurate statements about reality. Consequently, they believe that inerrancy asks the wrong questions of the text.[63] For inerrantists, none of these proposals take seriously enough the Bible's own claims to its being God's Word, bearing His unimpeachable authority in every area it addresses and in every claim it makes (and it does make claims!).

Second, how have defenders of inerrancy fared in this debate? Often throughout church history, theological controversy has brought about greater theological precision in restatements of traditional doctrines. This is certainly the case with the doctrine of inerrancy. The debates have produced a number of careful and sophisticated writings explaining and defending inerrancy. A notable example has been the work of the International Council on Biblical Inerrancy (formed in 1977), which drafted a fine statement of inerrancy (the "Chicago Statement on Biblical Inerrancy" in 1978) and which spurred the work of scholars in further clarification and defense of inerrancy.[64] Beyond this, supporters have not been stymied by ongoing discussions of "phenomena" that allegedly deny inerrancy. In the present era, then, evangelical scholars committed to inerrancy have flourished, even as they continue to refine their understanding of the doctrine of inerrancy and explore its implications.

Third, has inerrancy changed in any serious ways since the days of Warfield? Not in essence, though different emphases have occurred. Consider two examples. The first concerns how inerrantists have continued to respond to higher criticism. This is an important question since many of the methods of higher criticism have changed dramatically since Warfield's day. Some inerrantists today continue to oppose higher criticism as entirely incompatible with inerrancy. But others suggest that, when used cautiously and shorn of its anti-supernatural and anti-inerrancy assumptions, some historical-critical methods have limited utility. For example, Carson argues that a certain form of a critical method in Gospel studies known as "redaction criticism" may be of some limited help in better understanding a particular Gospel writer's emphasis, without in any way denying the historicity of his account.[65]

A second example of shifting emphases has to do with the whole question of Scripture's diverse literary genres. The Princetonians were, of course, well aware that Scripture has various literary types and that it makes ample use of figurative language, so that one should not interpret every statement of Scripture in a literalistic manner and claim that interpretation as inerrant. One would not, for example, read Jesus' statement that He is the vine (John 15:1) so literally as to claim that it is asserting inerrantly that Jesus is made a plant! What is inerrant is what Scripture actually affirms in the way it affirms it. Yet inerrantists today have paid even greater attention to Scripture's various literary genres. Kevin Vanhoozer has pointed out that the literature of Scripture does many things besides assert inerrant truth claims, though whenever Scripture does make assertions, it is always inerrant.[66] Although genre study has been applied by some in controversial ways,[67] it nevertheless is healthy because it forces us to pay closer attention to the text of Scripture, to better understand what

Scripture is actually claiming, and to appreciate the beauty and variety of its literature.

3. God's Word still communicates truth.

In many ways, this area of biblical authority has come under the greatest attack today. In no small measure, this heightened attack is due to the impact of postmodernity on our culture. We have already seen that authority is not terribly popular in our postmodern culture. But beyond that, postmodernism has affected biblical authority in at least two ways.

First, postmodernity, in its more radical expressions, denies objective meaning in a text. It rejects what has been normally assumed, that the meaning of a text is what the author intended to communicate in that text. For radical postmodernists, no text has an objective meaning, and any claim that it does is little more than one reader's attempt to gain power over other readers. Instead, meaning is determined by the individual reader or the community of readers of which one is a part.[68]

The impact of this is devastating to biblical authority: without any objective meaning to a biblical text, there is no *authoritative* text. As Vanhoozer puts it, "If there is no meaning in the text, then there is nothing to which the reader can be held accountable."[69] In reality, God has not really spoken—certainly He has not spoken to us. The serpent's question in the garden (Gen. 3:1) is given a new postmodern twist: "Did God really say [anything]?"[70] But the fundamental premise in the Bible is that God has spoken, that people are responsible for what God has said in the Word (e.g., 2 Kings 17:7–23), and that those who create their own meaning from Scripture distort the Word to their own detriment (e.g., 2 Peter 3:16).

Postmodernity has impacted biblical authority in a second way, particularly among some evangelicals. We saw earlier that the Princetonians emphasized the truth-telling function of Scripture: the Bible communicates true information. Since then, evangelicals have talked about the same thing by using the term "propositional revelation." What they are trying to safeguard is the idea "that revelation discloses truth in a cognitive manner."[71] It is this cognitive truth that must provide the foundation for what we believe and teach, and such truth is to be believed and taught by all believers.

But this commitment to propositional revelation runs counter to the postmodern ethos. Consequently, some evangelicals suggest that we need to rethink our understanding of biblical authority for a postmodern age. They make three points. First, we should think less about the Bible's authority in terms of the truth it communicates, and more in terms of what God uses Scripture to do in the community of the faithful. We should, for instance, emphasize the narrative of Scripture, because when the biblical stories become our own, they affect the way we view the world and live in it. Second, we should stop trying to build our theological beliefs on the sure foundation of propositional revelation in Scripture. Such a search for timeless truths and doctrinal certainty does not adequately recognize that all Christians are thoroughly enmeshed in a particular tradition, culture, and time. Third, we should therefore seek to think and live from within the perspective of our particular Christian community and "not pretend to have a universal perspective," that is, an "objective, absolute truth 'out there' that can be viewed objectively from 'nowhere.'"[72]

Conservative evangelicals might respond to this postmodern challenge in several ways. First of all, we have already seen that the Bible does do more than assert truths. Its narratives shape us; its poetry inspires us; its proverbs foster in us successful living; its prophecies instill fear of God in the present and hope for the future. But none of these functions is easily separated from Scripture's truth-telling function, nor should any be. Indeed, the fact that Scripture teaches truth adds force to Scripture's other functions in the life of the church.

In addition, it is true that all of us bring baggage to the interpretive process. Good biblical interpretation requires hard work, an attitude of humility and self-examination, and an openness to listen to the insights of others who might disagree with our interpretation. But though fair interpretation is difficult, it is not impossible. For if God has spoken, then meaning and truth must be accessible. And if God's truth is accessible, it should provide a basis for our theology if we want it to be based on revelation.

Furthermore, while human statements of theological truth will always reflect the theologian's culture and time, it is nevertheless possible to maintain that we are stating universal truth. It is important to distinguish between the timeless truths of Scripture communicated in the inspired words of Scripture and human expressions of those truths in theological statements. Human theological statements can state biblical truth, and they should strive for that, but they must never be equated with biblical truth as expressed by the words of Scripture. At the same time, Alister McGrath reminds us that doctrinal formulations can be considered "reliable, yet incomplete descriptions of reality." Hence, theologians regularly "reformulate, amplify or supplement a doctrine in response to changing historical circumstances."[73] Doctrinal formulations can thus change while still being true.

In the face of postmodernity, therefore, conservative evangelicals continue to insist that truth is accessible because God really has communicated in His Word. And because they believe it is a *concursive* (i.e., divine and human) Word, conservative evangelicals continue to affirm the absolute centrality of historical-grammatical exegesis. They certainly recognize that it is hard work and that presuppositions can make it difficult to gain an accurate understanding of what the text actually teaches. But they are convinced that the effort is well worth it, for it is this kind of exegesis that helps us to understand what God was saying through the human author, and through that, what He is saying to us today.

4. God's Word still communicates to us.

D. A. Carson reminds us that "reflective Christians . . . have always said that the Bible is not simply a book of facts: however many facts it contains, Scripture's purpose is not simply to fill our heads with facts, but to bring us to the living God."[74] The Holy Spirit's work did not end with inspiration. In His ongoing work of illumination, He continues to help us to understand and value His Word and bring it to bear in our lives so that we would ever increasingly come to know God better and be conformed to the image of Christ. As we saw with the Princetonians and other Protestants before them, the Spirit continues to use and empower the Word of God in the ongoing life of the church. Evangelicals are committed today to the same thing: the Bible is God's Word *to us*.

We must remember, however, that the Spirit uses Scripture in a way consistent with His work of inspiration. Put differently, His illuminating work is consistent with the meaning of the biblical text. This is important because some evangelicals are inclined in their devotionals and Bible studies to ignore what the human author was communicating in his context, the very meaning for which historical-grammatical exegesis searches. In our zeal to find what God is communicating to us today, we are tempted to bypass what the Spirit said through the human author. This has at least two problems. The first is that, in effect, it abandons the concursive nature of inspiration by not recognizing the truly human character of the text. But while God does speak to us through the text, He does so precisely through a text written through human authors centuries ago. The second problem with bypassing exegesis is that it ironically undercuts biblical authority. While people who do this may mean well, they often end up trying to make the text say what it really is not saying. The result can be little different from postmodern approaches to interpretation, where a text means whatever the reader wants it to mean. In such cases, we are transforming the text rather than allowing the text to transform us. But the Spirit's power is unleashed in God's Word precisely when it is rightly understood.

We must also remember that, because the Bible is the inspired, authoritative Word of God that the Spirit continues to use in His church, it must play a crucial role in the life of the church. This is why evangelicalism has been eager to get the Bible into the hands of as many as possible, so that each person can read the Word for herself or himself. Evangelicalism's concern for an accurate text (textual criticism) and its leadership in translating the Bible into all human languages and in improving upon already existing translations also reflect this conviction.[75] Furthermore, in its best expressions, evangelicalism continues to seek to keep the Bible at the center of church life and to recognize its sufficiency for that life. Our church services focus on the preaching of the Word; our songs put Scripture words and truths to music; we memorize Scripture; we study it regularly both individually and in groups; we read it to the sick, hurting, and bereaved, who find great comfort therein. The very life of the church is nourished by the authoritative Word of God empowered by His Spirit.

BIBLICAL AUTHORITY TODAY: PRACTICAL RAMIFICATIONS

American evangelicals today are a very practical group. Consequently, they are often preoccupied with the practical ramifications of doctrines, probably overly so and certainly not always for their own good.[76] Still, the question of doctrine's practicality is a good one to ask because important doctrines do have practical implications. What are the ramifications of our commitment to biblical authority? Consider just a few of these.

First, this evangelical conception of biblical authority affects *how we handle the Bible.* If I take seriously the idea that God has spoken, I can remain confident that the text has an accessible meaning, postmodernity notwithstanding. If I recognize that God has spoken through human authors, I will seek to base any application of the text on the author's intended meaning. If I believe that the Bible is God's Word, I will handle it with great care and will greatly value it. If I am convinced that the Holy Spirit continues to use the Word, I will eagerly listen to it when it is read or when a preacher proclaims its message, I will associate myself with ministries committed to the Scriptures, and I will seek the life-giving nourishment of the Word.

Second, our conception of biblical authority justifies *why we trust the Bible.* As God's Word, it is every bit as trustworthy as He is. This is why we trust the message of Scripture instead of the host of competing voices in our pluralistic world. This is why we seek only to understand Scripture instead of subjecting it to human evaluation to determine if what it says can really be believed. This is why we go to Scripture again and again when we desperately need to hear a word from the Lord.

Third, our strong view of the Scripture's authority influences *how I understand myself.* If I recognize that the Bible is the final, inerrant authority, I will not place my own judgment over the Bible. Instead, I will recognize my limitations and sinfulness and humbly place myself under Scripture's authority. Moreover, if I allow God's Word to sit in judgment of me, I will be in a better position to recognize how my own judgments have been shaped by the thought patterns of the world and to allow those judgments to be transformed by the renewing authority of the Word (cf. Rom. 12:1–2).

Finally, a commitment to full biblical authority relates to *how I understand God.* Because of His incredible mercy and grace, God has condescended to speak to us in ways we can understand. Because of His complete power, He is able to communicate to us effectively. Because of His faithfulness, trustworthiness, and omniscience, He does not make mistakes in what He says. Because of His justice, the consequences of not heeding His Word are fearful. Because of His love, He continues to speak to us today through His Word. Because of His infinite majesty, I am called to humbly submit to His Word. In short, this doctrine brings glory to God by highlighting the manifold greatness of His character.

God has spoken infallibly to us by the inspiration of His Spirit through human writers. That gives His Word the highest authority. It also makes it exceedingly precious, as David reminds us: "The law from your mouth is more precious to me than thousands of pieces of silver and gold" (Ps. 119:72).

NOTES

1. Millard J. Erickson, *Christian Theology*, 2d ed. (Grand Rapids: Baker, 1998), 268.
2. This distinction is discussed in Louis Igou Hodges, "New Dimensions in Scripture," *New Dimensions in Evangelical Thought: Essays in Honor of Millard J. Erickson*, ed. David S. Dockery (Downers Grove, Ill.: InterVarsity, 1998), 220–21. David Kelsey has similarly distinguished between thinking of scriptural authority as a property of the text versus seeing it as a function of the text in his important work *The Uses of Scripture in Recent Theology* (Philadelphia: Fortress , 1975).
3. Millard Erickson makes the point that "evangelical biblical scholars have been leaders in the practice of this area of criticism." See Millard J. Erickson, *The Evangelical Left: Encountering Postconservative Evangelical Theology* (Grand Rapids: Baker, 1997), 72.
4. J. Barton Payne, "Higher Criticism and Biblical Inerrancy," in *Inerrancy*, ed. Norman L. Geisler (Grand Rapids: Zondervan, 1980), 86. Payne even suggests that the term "higher criticism," which usually has negative connotations for conservatives because of its association with the historical-critical method, may be understood as only involving inquiry into "the circumstances of [a biblical book's] composition," including issues of authorship, date, genre, etc. Therefore, "when a person asks, 'Who wrote the Epistle to the Hebrews?' he is a higher critic!" Similarly, Mark Noll points out that the conservative evangelical scholars who opposed higher criticism in the late nineteenth century still considered themselves to be critical scholars because "they, like most academics in nineteenth-century America, regarded the careful, inductive, scientific sifting of evidence as the royal road to truth." What they opposed was a criticism biased against the supernatural character of Scripture. See Mark A. Noll, *Between Faith and Criticism: Evangelicals, Scholarship, and the Bible in America*, 2d ed. (Grand Rapids: Baker, 1991), 23.
5. Grant Wacker describes historical consciousness as "the belief that culture is the product of its own history, that ideas, values, and institutions of every sort are wholly conditioned by the historical setting in which they exist." Grant Wacker, "The Demise of Biblical Civilization," *The Bible in America: Essays in Cultural History*, ed. Nathan O. Hatch and Mark A. Noll (New York: Oxford Univ. Press, 1982), 125.

6. A concise but very helpful survey of the origins of biblical criticism in the sixteenth and seventeenth centuries can be found in John Woodbridge, *Biblical Authority: A Critique of the Rogers/McKim Proposal* (Grand Rapids: Zondervan, 1982), chap. 5.

7. For a survey of the history of higher criticism, see Gerald Bray, *Biblical Interpretation: Past and Present* (Downers Grove, Ill.: InterVarsity, 1996), part 2.

8. The most famous of these is the series of articles appearing between 1881 and 1883 in *The Presbyterian Review,* debating the compatibility between higher criticism and inspiration. For a discussion of this debate, see Roger Nicole's introduction in A. A. Hodge and B. B. Warfield, *Inspiration,* ed. Roger R. Nicole (Grand Rapids: Baker, 1979), xii–xiii, and Noll, *Between Faith and Criticism,* 15–27.

9. Noll estimates that almost one-third of the articles in *The Fundamentals* dealt with Scripture, and most of these sought to support its trustworthiness "against the methods, assumptions, and conclusions of what by that time was becoming the critical orthodoxy." Noll, *Between Faith and Criticism,* 39.

10. Wacker, "The Demise of Biblical Civilization," 124–25.

11. These categories are adapted from Noll, *Between Faith and Criticism,* chapters 2–3.

12. Those claiming the Princetonians had rejected the central tradition of the church on biblical authority include Jack B. Rogers and Donald K. McKim in *The Authority and Interpretation of the Bible* (San Francisco: Harper & Row, 1979); and Ernest Sandeen, *The Roots of Fundamentalism* (Chicago: Univ. of Chicago,1970). Their arguments are countered effectively by John Woodbridge in *Biblical Authority* and by Woodbridge and Randall H. Balmer, "The Princetonians and Biblical Authority: An Assessment of the Earnest Sender proposal," *Scripture and Truth,* ed. D. A. Carson and John Woodbridge (Grand Rapids: Zondervan, 1983), 251–79.

13. John Woodbridge, "Recent Interpretations of Biblical Authority, Part 4: Is Biblical Inerrancy a Fundamentalist Doctrine?" *Bibliotheca Sacra* 142 (October 1985): 301–2.

14. Hodge and Warfield carefully articulate the important role played by God's providential preparation of the Bible's human writers, though they clearly distinguish this preparation from inspiration, which presupposes such preparation but pertains to the process of writing itself. See Hodge and Warfield, *Inspiration,* 11–17, cf. Appendix 1.

15. See *The Inspiration and Authority of the Bible,* ed. Samuel G. Craig (Philadelphia: Presbyterian & Reformed, 1970), 154–58.

16. Some paleo-fundamentalists, like James Brookes, objected to the idea of "superintendence," at least early on, precisely because they believed that it was too indirect and passive a concept. See the discussion in David L. Saxon, "Fundamentalist Bibliology 1870–1900: An Analysis of the Paleo-Fundamentalist Views of Inspiration, Bible Translations, and Bible Criticism from the Writings of James H. Brookes, A. J. Gordon and A. T. Pierson" (Ph.D. diss., Bob Jones University, 1998), 66–68. See also Hodge and Warfield, *Inspiration,* 7, where they distinguish "superintendence" from "influence."

17. Warfield, *Inspiration and Authority,* 159.

18. Ibid., 133, cf. 154.

19. Ibid., 137.

20. B. B. Warfield, "The Inerrancy of the Original Autographs," ed. Mark A. Noll, *The Princeton Theology: 1812-1921: Scripture, Science, and Theological Method from Archibald Alexander to Benjamin Breckinridge Warfield,* 2d ed. (Grand Rapids: Baker, 2001), 269–74.

21. See Warfield, *Inspiration and Authority*, 134. Helpful contemporary discussions of this passage that come to the same conclusions include Paul Feinberg, "The Meaning of Inerrancy," in *Inerrancy*, ed. Norman L. Geisler (Grand Rapids: Zondervan, 1980), 277–83; and George W. Knight III, *The Pastoral Epistles: A Commentary on the Greek Text* (Grand Rapids: Eerdmans, 1992), 444-50.

22. See Hodge and Warfield, *Inspiration*, 18–23.

23. Warfield, *Inspiration and Authority*, 149.

24. Hodge and Warfield, *Inspiration*, 23.

25. See D. A. Carson, "Recent Developments in the Doctrine of Scripture," *Heremeneutics, Authority, and Canon*, ed. D. A. Carson and John D. Woodbridge (Grand Rapids: Zondervan, 1986), 29–30. For discussion of some paleo-fundamentalists on this point, see Saxon, "Fundamentalist Bibliology 1870–1900: An Analysis of the Paleo-Fundamentalist Views," 64–78.

26. Hodge and Warfield, *Inspiration*, 18–20; B. B. Warfield, "The Divine and Human in the Bible," *Princeton Theology*, 276. See also Charles Hodge, "Inspiration," in *Princeton Theology*, 139.

27. Warfield, "Divine and Human," *Princeton Theology*, 276–78.

28. Ibid., 279.

29. Warfield, *Inspiration and Authority*, 151–52.

30. Ibid., 138–46. A helpful contemporary description of Jesus' view of Scripture can be found in John W. Wenham, "Christ's View of Scripture," *Inerrancy*, 2–36.

31. Noll, *Princeton Theology*, 26 (esp. n. 40).

32. Warfield, *Inspiration and Authority*, 113.

33. Ibid., 112–13.

34. The term "infallible" has often been used throughout history to mean roughly the same thing as "inerrancy." However, inerrantists have come to prefer the term "inerrancy" because some have used the term "infallibility" to mean that Scripture does not deceive nor can it fail in matters pertaining to faith and practice, though it may have some "incidental" errors. See the discussion in Paul D. Feinberg, "The Meaning of Inerrancy," *Inerrancy*, 287–88.

35. Paul D. Feinberg, "Bible, Inerrancy and Infallibility of," in *Evangelical Dictionary of Theology*, ed. Walter A. Elwell (Grand Rapids: Baker, 1984), 142. All these elements can be seen in Hodge and Warfield, *Inspiration*, and in Warfield, *Inspiration and Authority*.

36. Warfield, *Inspiration and Authority*, 173.

37. Hodge and Warfield, *Inspiration*, 27–29, 30. They write (28–29): "There is a vast difference between exactness of statement, which includes an exhaustive rendering of details, and absolute literalness, which the Scriptures never profess, and accuracy, on the other hand, which secures a correct statement of fact or principles intended to be affirmed."

38. Ibid., 40.

39. See Warfield, *Inspiration and Authority*, 183–84.

40. Ibid., 139.

41. See the summary and bibliography in Noll, *Faith and Criticism*, 19–20; 229–30, notes 28–29.

42. These views are discussed by Warfield in several places. E.g., Warfield, *Inspiration and Authority*, 108, 169–70, 201ff.

43. Woodbridge, *Biblical Authority*, 21.

44. Warfield, *Inspiration and Authority*, 195.

45. See similar arguments against accommodation in Warfield, *Inspiration and Authority*, 117–18, 189–95.

46. Ibid., 171, cf. 121–22.
47. Timothy P. Weber, "The Two-Edged Sword: The Fundamentalist Use of the Bible," *The Bible in America,* ed. Hatch and Noll, 111, 113.
48. See Hodge and Warfield, *Inspiration,* 42, 44; Warfield, *Inspiration and Authority,* 120, 181–82.
49. This point has been emphasized in more contemporary analyses of the Princetonians. See, for example, Kelsey, *The Uses of Scripture,* 29–30, 32; and Stanley J. Grenz, *Renewing the Center: Evangelical Theology in a Post-Theological Era* (Grand Rapids: Baker, 2000), 71–77.
50. Hodge and Warfield, *Inspiration,* 43. Their statement here was intended to clarify that inerrancy applies to the human author's intended meaning consistent with the genre he used.
51. Warfield makes an interesting point in this regard. He claims even the allegorical method of interpretation used at times throughout church history demonstrated the allegorizers' conviction that the Bible is God's Word. Of course, Warfield considered allegorizing to be a "spurious daughter" of such reverence for the divine Word, presumably because it does not take concursis seriously. See Warfield, *Inspiration and Authority,* 109.
52. Ibid., 158–59.
53. Hodge and Warfield, *Inspiration,* 15.
54. Warfield, *Inspiration and Authority,* 161.
55. Warfield, "Divine and Human," *Princeton Theology,* 279. Cf. Warfield's remarkable description of the impact of Scripture in the church in Warfield, *Inspiration and Authority,* 106–7.
56. Hodge and Warfield, *Inspiration,* xiv.
57. See Gerald Bray, *Biblical Interpretation: Past and Present* (Downers Grove, Ill.: InterVarsity, 1996), 555–56. For example, Wayne Grudem, *Systematic Theology: An Introduction to Biblical Doctrine* (Grand Rapids: Zondervan, 1994), part 1; Erickson, *Christian Theology,* chaps. 10–11.
58. One thinks, for example, of some of the more radical participants of the Third Quest for the Historical Jesus, the most notorious of which has been the "Jesus Seminar." For an evangelical critique of the Jesus Seminar, see *Jesus Under Fire,* ed. Michael J. Wilkins and J. P. Moreland (Grand Rapids: Zondervan, 1995). For a helpful survey of the Third Quest, from more conservative to the quite radical, see Ben Witherington III, *The Jesus Quest: The Third Search for the Jew of Nazareth* (Downers Grove, Ill.: InterVarsity, 1997).
59. For a helpful discussion of this point, see D. A. Carson, *The Difficult Doctrine of the Love of God* (Wheaton, Ill.: Crossway, 2000), chapter 4.
60. George Marsden has thoroughly recounted the history of the initial breakup of this evangelical consensus at Fuller Seminary in George M. Marsden, *Reforming Fundamentalism: Fuller Seminary and the New Evangelicalism* (Grand Rapids: Eerdmans, 1987). For polemic and rhetorical reasons, a number of these have retained the term "inerrancy" even though they have modified its meaning.
61. Noll, *Princeton Theology,* 268.
62. For these views, see the discussion in Erickson, *Christian Theology,* 248–50; cf. Hodges, "New Dimensions in Scripture," *New Dimensions,* 212–13.
63. This approach seems to be exemplified in Clark Pinnock, "New Dimensions in Theological Method," *New Dimensions,* 197–208.
64. A copy and explanation of the Chicago Statement can be found in R. C. Sproul, *Explaining Inerrancy: A Commentary* (Oakland: ICBI, 1980). Other exemplary

works on inerrancy include *Inerrancy; Scripture and Truth;* and *Hermeneutics, Authority, and Canon.*

65. D. A. Carson, "Redaction Criticism: On the Legitimacy and Illegitimacy of a Literary Tool," *Scripture and Truth,* ed. Carson and Woodbridge (Grand Rapids: Zondervan, 1983), 140.

66. Kevin J. Vanhoozer, "The Semantics of Biblical Literature: Truth and Scripture's Diverse Literary Forms," *Hermeneutics, Authority, and Canon,* ed. D. A. Carson and John D. Woodbridge (Grand Rapids: Zondervan, 1986), 53–104. Cf. D. A. Carson, *The Gagging of God: Christianity Confronts Pluralism* (Grand Rapids: Zondervan, 1996), 163–74.

67. For example, some evangelicals have appealed to literary genre to deny certain traditional views, such as the historicity of Jonah (i.e., this is a parable, not historical) or the Pauline authorship of the Pastoral Letters (i.e., these are pseudonymous, which, they claim, is a common ancient literary genre).

68. For a summary of radical postmodern hermeneutics, see Carson, *Gagging of God,* chap. 3.

69. Kevin J. Vanhoozer, *Is There a Meaning in This Text? The Bible, the Reader, and the Morality of Literary Knowledge* (Grand Rapids: Zondervan, 1998), 86.

70. Note the discussion in Vanhoozer, "Semantics," *Hermeneutics, Authority, and Canon,* 63.

71. Ibid., 59.

72. Pinnock, "Theological Method," 203; cf. 200–207 for a description of this postmodern position, which he calls "simple biblicism." It is quite similar to the description of what Roger Olson has called "postconservative" evangelicalism. See Roger E. Olson, "Postconservative Evangelicals Greet the Postmodern Age," in *The Christian Century* 112 (3 May 1995): 480–83. A leading voice in postmodern evangelicalism is Stanley Grenz. For his approach, see Grenz, *Renewing the Center.*

73. Alister McGrath, "An Evangelical Evaluation of Postliberalism," ed. Timothy R. Phillips and Dennis L. Okholm, *The Nature of Confession: Evangelicals and Postliberals in Conversation* (Downers Grove, Ill.: InterVarsity, 1996), 30.

74. Carson, *Gagging of God,* 167.

75. See Bray, *Biblical Interpretation,* 561.

76. For example, many evangelicals are convinced of a certain doctrine's importance only when they can see the practical difference a doctrine makes. But David Wells argues that the evangelical church's pragmatic bent has had serious consequences because it has not taken theology itself seriously enough. See David Wells, *No Place for Truth, or Whatever Happened to Evangelical Theology?* (Grand Rapids: Eerdmans, 1993).

David Finkbeiner is associate professor of theology at the Moody Bible Institute. He received his Ph.D. degree in systematic theology at Trinity Evangelical Divinity School, Deerfield, Illinois, and has academic degrees from Bob Jones University, Greenville, South Carolina, and Biblical Theological Seminary, Hatfield, Pennsylvania.

3

JESUS CHRIST THE CORNERSTONE

CONCEIVED BY GOD
AND BORN OF A WOMAN

Robert K. Rapa

There was a time when most people believed that God had provided for humanity's basic needs through natural laws implemented at Creation. The familiar rhythms of sunrise and sunset, seedtime and harvest were viewed as evidence of a loving Creator who continued to provide for the lives of His creation and to order the affairs of His creatures. When the modern era arrived, however, the role of provider for and sustainer of humanity was largely given over to science. Many people came to believe that the universe was a closed system, governed by the natural law of cause and effect and in which an all-powerful God had no place. They expected science rather than God to provide answers to humanity's most profound questions and placed their hope in technological progress.

On the surface, such confidence might seem to have been warranted. Advances in medicine, food production, transportation, communication, and even household appliances have allowed many to enjoy an unequaled level of prosperity. Yet despite this progress, people continue to face the same problems that have plagued humanity's existence from the very beginning.

The complexities of life, bound up in birth and death, planting and harvesting, age and sickness, warfare and injustice, continue to be a part of our collective experience. Science and technology have not reduced our dependence upon the earth's food-producing capacity. Nor have they been able to eliminate our dependence upon favorable climactic conditions for such production. Science and technology have not been able to guarantee our collective welfare or provide us with the key to a harmonious existence. They have failed to deliver humankind from its desperate struggle for survival. Ironically, the twenty-first-century city dweller is as tied to the earth and the harsh realities of life as were the agrarian and nomadic peoples of the ancient world.

As a result, some have begun to question the promise of science and technology to offer progress and provide a better world for all. The modern age has given way to the postmodern era— an age in which rationalism is viewed as bankrupt, and the ideal of absolute truth has been replaced by the conviction that truth is a personal matter, not open to objective verification.

Science, entrusted with humanity's hope for rescue from its vulnerability to life's harsh realities, has failed to deliver in any ultimate sense. This has left many uneasy about life and the future. When modernism eliminated God from its worldview, it created a moral vacuum that science could not fill. The failure of science to produce the utopia modernism had expected has left postmodern people with a hopelessness that can only be countered by the dynamic message of the person, word, and work of Jesus Christ.

Through the virgin birth of Jesus of Nazareth, God became human. The Creator became a Creature, in order to deliver humanity from the meaninglessness and depravity that were the result of its own sinful rebellion. Far from being a story designed to perpetuate myth, this doctrine expresses the commitment of the Creator God to His creatures who were originally made in His image.[1] People struggling in the midst of life's pressures, or those looking for meaning or purpose, discover in the narrative of Jesus' incarnation the understanding that God is greater than life's problems. He is a faithful and beneficent Creator, able to accomplish His purposes for His creation.

For both disillusioned moderns and uncertain postmoderns, the doctrine of the virgin birth of the Lord Jesus brings comfort and hope. It is therefore a word for our times. In what follows, we will survey the church's commitment to this doctrine through the ages. We will suggest that the teaching of the Virgin Birth is one way to address humanity's difficulties. We hope, as well, to provide an argument for the continuing relevance of this doctrine for the life of the church of Jesus Christ and for the church's ongoing proclamation of Jesus as Lord of all.

THE DOCTRINE OF THE VIRGIN BIRTH IN THE HISTORY OF THE CHURCH

The doctrine of the Virgin Birth is not a new teaching, designed to reinforce a given faith community's perception of who Jesus was or is. Nor is it the idiosyncratic teaching of some aberrant faction of the church. There is continuity between what the modern evangelical church affirms that the Bible teaches about Jesus Christ and what was held to be true about Him by the first Christians. This continuity may be found in a "stream of tradition" flowing from the earliest period of the church to our own day. In fact, as Machen has suggested, the aberrant factions of the church were those that denied the Virgin Birth, which was from earliest times included in the formulation of "essential Christian belief . . . of the Church at large."[2]

From the beginning, the church has universally affirmed that Jesus of Nazareth, as the words of an ancient creed of the church of Rome declared, was "born by the Holy Ghost of the Virgin Mary." Dating from about the middle of the second century, this creed attested to the early church's understanding of the supernatural origin of Jesus of Nazareth.[3] His birth was unique, the result of a "divine-human cooperative" between God the Holy Spirit and His willing servant Mary. Jesus' birth was not the result of normal human biology; it was a direct creative act of God the Holy Spirit, whereby He formed in the womb of Mary the humanity of the Lord Jesus (Isa. 7:14; Matt. 1:18–25; Luke 1:26–38).[4]

The Old Roman Creed (an early version of the Nicene Creed) was formulated as a baptismal statement of faith to indicate what minimum truths must be confessed in order to gain visible entrance into the church. It included language that refuted both the denial of Jesus' physical human existence as found, for example, in docetism, an early heresy that claimed that Jesus' body was not real. The creed was also meant to refute those who denied Christ's deity, like the Ebionites, a Jewish/Christian hybrid that observed the Mosaic Law and rejected the writings of the apostle Paul. The Old Roman Creed served as the basis for the Apostles' Creed, which in its earliest form itself is believed to have dated from about the year 200, and was the forerunner of other church creeds, as well.

Additional information regarding the Virgin Birth from this period of church history is found in the writings of early church fathers, such as Justin Martyr's *Dialogue with Trypho* (*Dialogue* [D.] 43, 66). Justin attempted to prove to Trypho, who was a Jew, that Jesus was the fulfillment of the Hebrew Scriptures. In the process he answered many Jewish objections to the Virgin Birth and to Jesus' identity as Messiah.[5] Ignatius of Antioch, another early father, mentions the Virgin Birth in his *Epistle to the Ephesians* (D. 18–19; cf. also 7, 20) and *Epistle to the Smyrneans* (D. 20). In the latter *Epistle,* he praises the Smyrneans for their faith, and especially for their belief in the Virgin Birth.

This particular reference is important, because Ignatius wrote this epistle to refute the error of docetism. He would only have had to mention Jesus' birth "of a woman" to prove His true humanity. The fact that he mentioned the Virgin Birth, rather than referring merely to a physical birth, gives added weight to the impression that Ignatius, like Justin and others in his time, assumed the truth of the biblical accounts of Christ's birth.[6] These early references in the creeds and in the Fathers are significant, because they function as a defense of the doctrine of the Virgin Birth, as statements of faith, and sometimes are assumed as the means to advance other theological arguments in the Fathers' writings.[7] They demonstrate that the doctrine of the Virgin Birth was a foundational belief of the early church.[8]

The Reformers, too, believed and taught that the virgin birth of Christ was an essential component of Christianity. With regard to the Virgin Birth, Martin Luther wrote in *The Schmalkald Articles,* "The Son became a human being in this way: He was conceived by the Holy Spirit without male participation and was born of the . . . Virgin Mary." These *Articles* reveal Luther's "highest theological priorities."[9] So, the inclusion of the doctrine of the Virgin Birth at the very beginning of this body of material is a powerful indication of Luther's perception of this doctrine's importance. Calvin also discussed the Virgin Birth in his *Institutes of Christian Religion* (2.13, 1–3) but did so as an ancillary argument to his main purpose in writing. He addressed the Virgin Birth as a part of his treatment of the necessity for Christ to become human in order to fulfill His office as Mediator. In this discussion, Calvin demonstrated that Christ's "descent" through the Virgin Mary is not to be understood allegorically but that Jesus did in fact take on true humanity, in accord with the biblical accounts. In its context, his argument is nonsensical if Jesus was not born "of a virgin."

More recently, it has been necessary for the church to defend the doctrine of the Virgin Birth against the anti-supernaturalism of higher criticism. Attacks against the supernatural elements of Christ's person and work are, of course, broader than the Virgin Birth. They are made against the biblical record of His earthly life, His claims to deity, His sinlessness, His miracles, and His resurrection from the dead. But, as noted by James Orr, writing in *The Fundamentals,* "the Virgin Birth is assailed with special vehemence, because it is supposed that the evidence for this miracle is more easily got rid of than the evidence for public facts." Orr then defended the traditional understanding of the Virgin Birth against such objections, showing the inadequacy of alternative explanations for Jesus' birth and life, and demonstrating that it is this traditional understanding, based upon the records of the Gospels' birth narratives, that makes the best sense of all available evidence. Machen's *Virgin Birth* stands with Orr's piece as a magisterial contribution in this defense. Taken together, these works address relevant objections to or perversions of this doctrine, ancient or recent, whether arising out of an anti-supernaturalistic bias, supposed parallels to ancient Near Eastern hero-gods, or other questions of the biblical accounts.

The historical record is clear: The church has steadfastly maintained that Jesus Christ is the God-Man. He was born of the Virgin Mary by the Holy Spirit in a miraculous, divine creative act. The notion of Jesus having been born as one person with both divine and human natures surely entails "mystery," yet this is the foundation of the church's understanding of His uniqueness as the God-Man.[10] No human parents, sinful or otherwise, could produce a divine offspring. No human parents could give birth to God, who alone could remedy humanity's condition.[11] The doctrine of the Virgin Birth has from the beginning been woven into the warp and woof of Christianity. However, as important as the church's historical understanding of the Virgin Birth may be, its validity ultimately depends upon those documents that were the source of its understanding. What do the Scriptures say about the nature of Christ's birth? Moreover, what significance does this truth have for our lives and ministries?[12]

ISAIAH'S PREDICTION OF THE VIRGIN BIRTH

Isaiah's prophecy of the Virgin Birth came in the midst of political turmoil that resulted from Ahaz's sinful obstinacy (cf. 2 Kings 16:2–4; 2 Chron. 28:5) and the threat to his kingdom by Rezin, king of Aram (Syria), and Pekah, king of Israel (Isa. 7:1–2, 4–6).[13] Ahaz and all of Judah were in deep despair, threatened with destruction because Ahaz had refused to join with Rezin and Pekah in an alliance against Assyria. In an effort to assure Ahaz of His continued covenant presence, God sent the prophet Isaiah to speak to Ahaz and directed the prophet to take along his son Shear-jashub. The boy's presence, serving as a symbol of the next Israelite generation, and his name, which meant "a remnant will return," suggested that there would continue to be a future for God's covenant people (Isa. 7:3). Yahweh assured Ahaz of His presence in language that was reminiscent of the establishment of the Davidic Covenant and encouraged him to take seriously his position as shepherd of God's people by faithfully discharging his responsibilities as the agent of that covenant (vv. 4–9). To further assure the king, Yahweh commanded Ahaz to ask for a sign. The sign, of whatever nature Ahaz desired, was intended to confirm for Ahaz that Yahweh's word concerning the two kings would indeed come to pass (vv. 7–8, 11). Although Ahaz's refusal was cast in terms of religious piety, it was actually a further instance of obstinate disobedience (v. 12). As stated by Van Groningen,

The prompt but curt reply of Ahaz indicates his refusal to obey and trust in Yahweh. Ahaz chooses the way of unbelief; it is the sure way into a severe crisis for him and his people. Ahaz' choice is obvious: an alliance with Assyria and through it a victory, he hopes, over his enemies to the north. But Ahaz does not express his obvious reason for refusing to ask for a sign. Rather, he gives what could be said to be to be a biblical and religious reason . . . "I will not test Yahweh."[14]

Isaiah responded to Ahaz by addressing him as the "house of David," that is, in Ahaz's capacity as the representative of the Davidic Covenant (Isa. 7:13). Because of Ahaz's obstinacy, the Lord Himself gave a sign, not only to him but to the entire covenant nation. This sign was to be a "virgin" *(alma)* who conceives and gives birth to a son.[15] This son would be called "Immanuel," which means "God with us" or "God is with us." This startling pronouncement by Yahweh was intended to bring comfort and assurance to His covenant people. It was the promise of His abiding presence with and protection of His people, and specifically the Davidic dynasty, as demonstrated by the birth of a child. Indeed, this comfort would come *by virtue of* the birth of the child.

If the child's identity had meaning for Ahaz and the people of Judah in Isaiah's day, the prophecy may have referred to Isaiah's second son, Maher-shalal-hash-baz. He was born to Isaiah and "the prophetess" shortly after Isaiah's pronouncement to Ahaz (cf. Isa. 8:1–16). His birth would fit the criteria of Isa. 7:14–16, if it is assumed that the prophetess was a virgin before conceiving this child. The child would have served as a "sign" of Yahweh's continued presence in both the prediction of his birth and as a result of the undoing of Rezin and Pekah in a timely fashion (cf. Isa. 8:4).

Another option for the identity of the child, if its identity was known to Ahaz and his contemporaries, is that a specific woman known to Ahaz and suspected by him to be pregnant (perhaps a member of his harem) actually was pregnant and would bear a son. By that time hope would have returned to Judah when the two kings that were now arrayed against Ahaz were finally defeated. It is also possible, of course, that this prophecy is a direct reference to the birth of Jesus, as recorded specifically by Matthew (1:18–25). This view has been popular among evangelicals. Its weakness, however, is that such an interpretation would not have had meaning for Ahaz and his contemporaries.[16]

It is unlikely that Isaiah fully understood how all of this would develop over time into Yahweh's covenant faithfulness to His people in and through His Son, the Lord Jesus.[17] Nevertheless, Isaiah's prophecy had import for Ahaz and Judah, in that God's Word was fulfilled for them. A child was born, and before that child matured Rezin and Pekah were destroyed. God had demonstrated His presence with, faithfulness to, and deliverance of His covenant people, just as He had promised. Matthew later saw a greater significance, both for the Davidic dynasty and the redemptive hopes of humanity, in Isaiah's prophecy of Immanuel and noted its ultimate fulfillment in the person of the greater David, Jesus of Nazareth (Matt. 1:22–23).

MATTHEW'S DESCRIPTION OF THE BIRTH OF CHRIST

Matthew's gospel is fulfillment oriented. He wrote to demonstrate that Jesus of Nazareth was the One in whom all the redemptive hopes and promises of the Hebrew Scriptures were bound up. To this end, Matthew uses variants of the term "to fulfill" *(plerow)* seventeen times in his Gospel, five times in the first two chapters alone. This suggests that Matthew crafted the birth narrative in these first two chapters specifically to demonstrate the manner in which Jesus "fills up" the redemptive history of Israel.

Matthew begins with Jesus' genealogy. Though he does not

use the word *fulfill* in these verses, he surely intended that we understand that Jesus fills up the significance of the Davidic Covenant. Matthew bases his genealogy on Old Testament "official" genealogical texts, most likely Chronicles.[18] Further, he structures the very first verse of the Gospel ("the book of the genealogy of Jesus Christ, the Son of David, the Son of Abraham") in a way that clearly denotes his intention. David is chronologically after Abraham, and normal protocol would have mentioned Abraham first, especially since he is regarded as the father of the entire nation. But Matthew has gone "out of his way" to name the descendant ahead of his greater ancestor, signaling the intent to tie Jesus in a particular way to King David.

Matthew's genealogy ties Jesus to David in other ways, as well. It uses David's name five times, and Matthew's summary comment at verse 17 seems to center Israel's history in David's reign. In addition, as Carson has pointed out, the repeated use of "fourteen generations" in this verse may also suggest "David," since the numerical equivalent of his name adds up to fourteen.[19]

But Matthew's genealogy does more than merely tie Jesus to David. He is also "Son of Abraham." Jesus is the fulfillment of the promise of God to Abraham that "in [his] seed all nations" would be blessed. Throughout the genealogy, Matthew's gospel hints at how this might be. Ancient genealogies seldom mentioned women, unless those women were highlighted for some outstanding contribution to the nation or were famous in some other way. The women listed in Jesus' genealogy, however, were not famous but "infamous." Tamar, Rahab, Ruth, and Bathsheba (who is not actually named but simply referred to as "she who was the wife of Uriah") were all non-Israelite women of questionable repute. Tamar had prostituted herself to Judah (Genesis 37–38). Rahab was a Cannanite harlot who was manipulative and untruthful (Joshua 2, 6). Ruth was honorable in her dealings but was a Moabitess. The Moabites were descended from the incestuous relationship between Lot and his daughter and cursed by Yahweh because they hired Balaam to curse Israel as she came out of Egypt (Gen. 19:30–37; Deut. 23:3–4). Bathsheba was involved with David in that horrible "Uriah incident," which included adultery, murder, and the later death of the child. No wonder Matthew didn't name her!

But Matthew was interested in demonstrating God's grace, both to Israel, as promised in the Davidic Covenant, and to "all nations," as promised in the Abrahamic Covenant. In addition, he was preparing the way for the next "infamous" woman in the genealogy: Mary. God had demonstrated in the history of Israel His ability to rule, and overrule in numerous instances, in order to further His redemptive purposes. The "questionable" women in Jesus' ancestry may not be the "kind" of women we might highlight in our backgrounds. But God extends grace to sinners and uses these women, "warts and all," to be the female progenitors of the Messiah, the redeemer of Israel and all people, in order to achieve His greatest redemptive act of all![20]

In this way, Matthew's gospel prepares the reader for Mary and the scandal of her pregnancy. "Before" she and Joseph "come together" (in sexual union at marriage), she "was found to be with child" (1:18).[21] Matthew then notes, "All this took place to fulfill what the Lord had said through the prophet"; and Matthew quotes Isaiah 7:14 and 8:8. In other words, Jesus' birth through a virgin exactly "fills up" Isaiah's predictive prophecy in ways that Isaiah could not have imagined but in which he would certainly approve. Jesus is "with us God," born of a virgin, in order that God's redemptive purposes would be met in Him.

The hopes of Israel (especially as expressed in terms of the Davidic Covenant in Isaiah 7–8, which Matthew quotes here), and all humanity, are bound up in the incarnation of God in the person of Jesus. He was born of the Virgin Mary because God purposed in Him to fulfill the Davidic and Abrahamic Covenants. In Jesus, God purposed to be "present" with His people Israel and to "bless" all nations through Him.

LUKE'S ACCOUNT OF THE BIRTH OF CHRIST

Luke's infancy narrative seems to assume much of the information Matthew relates but takes a somewhat different tack than that of Matthew by highlighting ways in which Jesus meets the needs of sinners. This is symbolized in his Gospel by the poor and disenfranchised.

Luke's gospel begins with Zacharias and Elizabeth, a priest married to a daughter of Aaron, both of whom Luke identified as "righteous" and "blameless." In other words, these were "good people," outstanding examples of covenant fidelity and obedience. But what the book of Luke grants in one sentence, it takes away with the next when it identifies the couple as "[having] no child, because Elizabeth was barren, and they were advanced in years" (Luke 1:7–8 NASB). To Luke's original readers this would have suggested that, despite their fine pedigrees, Zacharias's vocation as a priest, and appearances to the contrary, the couple had been cursed by God. Barrenness amounted to a scandalous situation in Israel, one that only God could remedy by removing the curse (cf. Gen. 15:2–6; 25:21–26; 29:31–30:24; 1 Sam. 1:1–20).[22] So, no matter their "official" position within Israel, others would have regarded this couple as "outsiders" to God's blessing, not part of His true people.

Mary, too, is portrayed as disenfranchised, though her disenfranchisement centers in her "sin," the fact that she is pregnant outside of marriage (Matt. 1:18–21; Luke 1:26–33). No "sinner" could be expected to receive approbation from God, and so Mary by default is considered to be outside the category of God's true people.

Yet in both instances, God has the last word. Zacharias and Elizabeth give birth to John the Baptist, the forerunner of the Messiah, whose ministry to the people of Israel will be effective unto repentance (Luke 1:15–18). God "visits" not only Zacharias and Elizabeth but through them and the ministry of their son, all Israel (Luke 1:15–18, 67–79). And Mary, though under a cloud of suspicion her entire life for her "illegitimate" pregnancy (cf. John 8:41), becomes the mother of the Lord Jesus, the Messiah of Israel and Savior of all humanity. The "Holy One" born of Mary is sinless, conceived supernaturally for the redemption of sinners (Luke 1:35). The designation "Holy One" literally meant "set apart," in this case meaning separate from sin.

The annunciation of the child's birth to shepherds further stresses God's concern for the oppressed (Luke 2:8–20). Shepherds, too, were considered "perpetually unclean," base fellows who were untrustworthy and shut out of "proper" society. God "reversed" the fortunes of these disenfranchised people, just as through their obedience to His Word, He reverses the fortunes of sinful humanity. In the persons of Zacharias and Elizabeth and Joseph and Mary, we see God working through otherwise unfortunate circumstances to achieve His purposes. God's purposes prove to be greater than those affected could even begin to hope.

Certainly barrenness is difficult, and Zacharias and Elizabeth were greatly relieved to have had the child for which they had desperately longed. Surely the social ostracism and shameful stigma associated with what appeared to others as her illegitimate pregnancy was hurtful to Mary. Joseph's marrying her despite her condition also brought him under suspicion. He would have been considered either to be the child's father himself, or as foolishly having married a woman who had been unfaithful to him. But God was at work to reclaim these circumstances and to bring about His answer, not just to these "apparent" problems but to humanity's greatest problem: the need for redemption. This could only come through the person and work of the God-Man, Jesus Christ. Luke masterfully has woven the truth of Jesus' virgin birth into the fabric of his Gospel in such a way as to point up God's great grace, displayed in His concern for even the lowliest members of society.

THE IMPACT OF THE VIRGIN BIRTH
ON THE LIVES OF BELIEVERS

The theological truths of the Virgin Birth speak powerfully to our lives as God's people. In many ways, these truths commend themselves to us as the means to strengthen our faith, encourage our hearts, and proclaim to others the hope of salvation in the person and work of the Lord Jesus. In what follows, we will draw out some of the practical implications of the doctrine of the Virgin Birth.

Grace and Humanity

The doctrine of the Virgin Birth speaks to us of God's commitment to His creation and to humanity as His creatures. God created us as persons in His own image for His own purposes (Genesis 1–2). People were not created "for themselves," or to be free from a relationship to God.

People were to understand their value and their worth, and find their dignity in terms of being creatures of the one true, living God and in their collective role as His vice-regents on the earth. But the relationship people were to have to God and to creation was circumscribed by His purposes (Gen. 1:26–2:3, 7, 15–25; Ex. 20:8). In violating those creation ordinances, Adam and Eve plunged themselves and the entire human race into wicked rebellion against God, resulting in utter despair and hopelessness. But because humanity was created in God's image, He would not abandon His creatures to suffer the result of their sinful rebellion. Nor would He allow the cosmos to suffer interminably the decay that accompanied the Fall. God intervened to orchestrate the overturning of human rebellion, and that intervention culminated in the Incarnation.

Jesus, God the Son, entered into human history through the Virgin Birth to accomplish the "undoing" of Adam's sin by living in perfect obedience to the Father and carrying out His will on behalf of fallen humanity. In His earthly life (which included His earthly ministry of obedience and works, His crucifixion and death, His resurrection, ascension, and sending the Holy Spirit at Pentecost), Jesus did for humanity what humanity could not do for itself. He recapitulated in His person and work both the history of Israel and the history of all humanity. As its representative, He died sacrificially for humanity's sin: "God made him who had no sin to be sin for us, so that in him we might become the righteousness of God" (2 Cor. 5:21). All creation will eventually be brought into proper relationship to God through Him (Rom. 8:18–25).

In all of this, we see the commitment of God to us as His children. He Himself entered into our existence so as to take upon Himself the penalty of our sinfulness and reclaim us for His purposes. This speaks powerfully of our value as people. Many today attempt to find value for themselves in what they do vocationally, or in amassing wealth, or in therapeutic models relating to "self-image." All of these pale in significance when we consider the value we have as image bearers of God. The church of Jesus Christ, by heralding the truths of God's grace to His creatures, can call people to a true appreciation of their value as reflections of God's image.

Grace and Humility

The doctrine of the Virgin Birth also teaches us that God is God and we are not. One component of our sinfulness is pride. We tend to think more of ourselves than we ought or we fail to see our brokenness and need. Much of the Bible speaks to this condition of fallen humanity, and we often underestimate the extent to which it has taken root in our lives.[23] We sometimes fail to understand or fully appreciate that we are completely dependent upon God to rectify our fallen condition. There is nothing we can do to change our status as sinners in His presence (Rom. 3:10–18, 23; 6:23; Eph. 2:8–9; Titus 3:5). Nor can we do anything on our own to please Him (Phil. 2:12–13). In fact, we often fail to appreciate that we are completely dependent upon God for every aspect of our existence (Matt. 6:25–34).

Here again the doctrine of the Virgin Birth helps us. Because we are completely dependent creatures, who must look to the gracious provision of our God for every need, He has come to us in the person of the Son to reconcile us to Himself. Jesus' life modeled dependency upon God. This lifestyle of dependency was reflected in His temptation, His performance of miracles "in the Spirit," and His determination to do only what the Father had given Him to do (John 5:19–27; 8:28–29). In His greatest recorded sermon, Jesus encouraged us to cultivate a childlike dependency upon our heavenly Father by practicing "poverty of spirit" (Matt. 5:3). Indeed, rightly interpreted, all of the Beatitudes speak of this dependency.

We are encouraged throughout the New Testament to become as little children, and are compared to sheep, in order to communicate the extent of this dependency. In the Incarnation, Jesus took upon Himself a human nature in order to identify with us in our vulnerability and to bring us out of rebellious self-reliance and back into a relationship of dependency upon our Creator God. As His children, we are to accomplish His will through obedience and service (cf. Luke 8:15; Eph. 2:10). By living out our dependence upon God, we as the church of Jesus Christ can live powerfully in His strength and for His purposes.

Grace and Obedience

The doctrine of the Virgin Birth teaches us that it is not always necessary to understand how God intends to accomplish His purposes in and through us. The people represented in the Bible narratives we have discussed were not fully aware of what

God was doing when He dealt with them. Their respective roles in preparing for the coming of the Messiah intersected with each other across hundreds of years and thousands of generations. Tamar, for example, could not have known that her pain and humiliation would eventually contribute to the fulfillment of God's promises to Israel in the person of Jesus Christ.

Isaiah, no doubt, was saddened at Ahaz's obstinate sinfulness. Yet God used that circumstance to remind them both of the reality of His presence and to predict and eventually bring about the fulfillment of the promise to Israel bound up in the Davidic Covenant through the virgin birth of Jesus. Elizabeth felt great shame and humiliation because of her barrenness and could not have anticipated in the long years of her suffering that God would use her to bear the forerunner of the Messiah.

Each of these people, despite years of pain, suffering, humiliation, misunderstanding, and confusion, were in some way instrumental in bringing about the birth of Jesus. God knew what He was doing in and through each of them, even if they themselves did not.

Thus the Virgin Birth should encourage us to trust our gracious God to work His purposes in and through our lives even though we do not fully understand what He is doing. Ours is but to "trust and obey" and to represent God faithfully in this world. The church of Jesus Christ does not need to have the "answer" to every existential question that may arise in each person's life. We are confident that in our Savior we have the Answer for the ages! Like Mary, we can respond to the exigencies of our lives by affirming, "May it be done to me according to your word!" (Luke 1:38 NASB).

Grace and Suffering

Closely related to this confidence is the knowledge that we can bear up under suffering. In bringing about the Virgin Birth,

God invaded the lives of numerous people without their "permission." He did this in spite of the fact that many of these people were put into positions of hardship, disgrace, and shame in order to bring about His purposes. Their trials, their feelings of abandonment by God, their experiences of social or religious disenfranchisement by others, were all due to "God's will" for their lives—even when they were unaware of it at the time.

The church needs to hear this word today! We do many things to surround ourselves with comfort and to avoid suffering. We often interpret suffering in the lives of others in just the same way that religious people around Zacharias and Elizabeth or Mary and Joseph did. We often believe that if we or someone else struggles or suffers, it is somehow because of God's curse.

We fall victim to what might be called "Maria Von Trapp" theology. In the movie account of this nun's life, "The Sound of Music," Maria responded with song when the captain asked her to marry him. "Nothing comes from nothing," she concluded, singing that the reason for this proposal from the man she loves is because sometime during her life, "I've must've done something good."

We too can fall prey to the mistaken notion that God balances His cosmic scales by some divine tit-for-tat equation. For every mistake or misdeed, we look for God's cosmic "flyswatter" to fall, squashing our spirit, flattening our hope, and smashing our joy—or, if we do something "good," to reward us.

The New Testament repeatedly teaches that our suffering has value, whether that suffering is due to persecution, or due to our identity as messianic people (Matt. 5:10–12; Rom. 5:3–5; Col. 1:24; 1 Peter 2:18–21; 4:12–14). We learn patience and gain victory through suffering (James 1:12–18; Rev. 2–3). It is in suffering that we become like the Master, who entered human experience and suffered humiliation and rejection, misunderstanding and persecution, deprivation and grief, and was horribly and wickedly slaughtered for our sinfulness. Let us not think that suffering is always the result of our failures and God's judgment (though, of course, that may at times be the case). God uses suffering to conform us to the image of His Son. Let us, as the church of Jesus Christ, welcome into our midst brothers and sisters who are broken and suffering, and together with our Savior let us bind up one another's wounds to the glory of God.

The doctrine of the Virgin Birth is a precious, time-honored teaching of the church. Though many may scoff at such teaching, believers have much to celebrate in the truths represented there. Our God is sovereign, powerful enough to both orchestrate and carry out His redemptive program across many centuries and through many generations. His commitment to His people and creation is met, despite human sin, weakness, failure, and resistance. God supernaturally invaded human history, accomplishing His purposes.

God did all this in and through people like us. He has accomplished His purposes in and through people for whom He cares and to whom He is fully committed. His commitment to humanity is a "commitment to death," the death of the God-Man, Jesus.

NOTES

1. There are many who reject the teaching of the Virgin Birth for a variety of reasons, most having to do with the rejection of the Bible as God's authoritative self-revelation or with the identification of Jesus of Nazareth as deity, or as the Jewish Messiah. The timeworn notion that Jesus' birth narratives as recorded in the canonical Gospels parallel and are indebted to ancient Mesopotamian myths or Hellenistic hero/god stories has been frequently recast and updated for mass digestion (as in stories about Jesus' birth and life in television documentaries or popular newsmagazines or on the Internet). Yet these supposed parallels, as well as early Jewish apologetic formulations against the Virgin Birth, have already been proved wanting by J. Gresham Machen, *The Virgin Birth of Christ* (1930; reprint, Grand Rapids: Baker, 1980). See also James Orr, "The Virgin Birth of Christ," in *The Fundamentals* (Chicago: Testimony Publishing Co., n.d.); and Robert G. Gromacki, *The Virgin Birth* (Nashville: Thomas Nelson, 1974).
2. Machen, *The Virgin Birth*, 3.
3. Robert L. Ferm, *Readings in the History of Christian Thought* (New York: Holt, Rinehart & Winston, 1964), 105ff.

4. As used here, "humanity" refers to Jesus' human person, i.e., His physical body and His human nature.

5. Justin Martyr, *Dialogue with Trypho*, Dialogue 43, 66. Citations of the apostolic Fathers are taken from Alexander Roberts and James Donaldson, eds., with A. Cleveland Coxe, *The Ante-Nicene Fathers* (Grand Rapids: Eerdmans, 1975).

6. In addition to the statements by Justin and Ignatius referenced here, other statements from the early church about the Virgin Birth may be found in Aristides *(Apology for the Christians to the Roman Emperor)*; Tatian *(Diatessaron; Address to the Greeks)*; Melito of Sardis *(Discourse on the Cross; Discourse on the Soul and Body; From Melito the Bishop, On Faith)*; Hippolytus *(Refutation of All Heresies; Treatise on Christ and Anti-Christ; On Proverbs XXIV; Against Beron and Helix)*; and Tertullian *(On the Flesh of Christ; The Prescription Against Heretics; Against Praxeas; Against Marcion;* and possibly in *The Shows)*. See Roberts and Donaldson, eds., *The Ante-Nicene Fathers* for the information contained in these primary sources.

7. Apologetic for the Virgin Birth in this time period occurs particularly in light of Jewish opposition to this teaching and against Gnostic denials of Jesus' true humanity. Origen, in his *Against Celsus* (early third century), addresses well some of these concerns. Celsus was a pagan philosopher who based his denial of the Virgin Birth on Jewish opposition to Christian teaching regarding Jesus. In this treatise, Origen persuasively refutes both Celsus's pagan thought and his "borrowed" Jewish reasoning against the doctrine of the Virgin Birth. Justin's earlier *Dialogue with Trypho* had addressed many of the same Jewish objections. Gnostic denials of Jesus' humanity by early Christian heretics such as Carpocrites and Cerinthus were refuted by Fathers like Irenaeus *(Against Heretics,* about A.D. 184).

8. The words of Machen are pertinent here, as he notes, "When we find [Ignatius] attesting the Virgin Birth not as a novelty but altogether as a matter of course, as one of the accepted facts about Christ, it becomes evident that the belief in the Virgin Birth must have been prevalent long before the close of the first century," in Machen, *Virgin Birth,* 7.

9. William R. Russell, *The Schmalkald Articles: Luther's Theological Testament* (Minneapolis: Fortress, 1995), ix. The quotation is from part 1, article 4.

10. On the Virgin Birth as "mystery," note especially Karl Barth, *Church Dogmatics,* (Edinburgh: T & T Clark, 1960) III.15.3.

11. See Kenneth S. Kantzer, "The Miracle of Christmas," *Christianity Today,* 14 December 1984, 15.

12. The exegetical task centered in the biblical accounts relative to the Virgin Birth cannot be fully explored here. The reader is referred to relevant commentaries and monographs on issues associated with the accounts in Isaiah, Matthew, Luke, and elsewhere in the New Testament (e.g., possible allusions to the Virgin Birth in John's prologue or Paul's writings).

13. For an excellent treatment of the background and interpretive details of this section, see Gerard Van Groningen, *Messianic Revelation in the Old Testament* (Grand Rapids: Baker, 1990), 521–37.

14. Van Groningen, *Messianic Revelation,* 527.

15. There is, of course, massive literature on the question of the precise translation of *alma* and its cognate, *betula,* and the resulting implications for the understanding of this passage. Many have staked out definite parameters of meaning for these terms, the first as definitely "virgin" (cf. J. Alec Motyer, *The Prophecy of Isaiah* [Downers Grove, Ill.: InterVarsity, 1993], 84–86), and the second as more generally "young woman" (cf. E. J. Young, *Studies in Isaiah* [Grand Rapids: Eerdmans,

1954], 161–63). However, on the basis of lexical evidence it is best to understand that both words can refer to either one, or both at the same time (that is, a "young woman" who also happens to be "virgin"; cf. John H. Walton, "Isaiah 7:14: What's in a Name?" *Journal of the Evangelical Theological Society* 30 [1987]: 289–306, esp. 291–93). Thus the question of the identity of Isaiah's *alma* cannot be decided on the basis of the word alone.

16. Evangelicals embracing this interpretation include J. Alec Motyer, E. J. Young, Robert L. Reymond *(Jesus, Divine Messiah)*, and J. Wash Watts *(Old Testament Teaching)*. However, this approach seems to be an attempt to interpret Isaiah through the lens of Matthew and may be driven more by theological than exegetical issues. Note here the discussion of Walton, "Isaiah 7:14," 293–99.

17. Of course, this is not to deny predictive or messianic prophecy. The Old Testament prophets may not have known fully all that their statements would come to mean, but they knew that theirs was a "divine word," a word from Yahweh, and therefore "had a cause-and-effect relationship with history" (Walton, "Isaiah 7:14," 299). As such they expected that further significance of their predictive word would unfold through time. In this way, they no doubt understood that their prophecies laid the groundwork for further redemptive-historical development, and that their words would not be contradicted by that later development but rather would be "filled up" by further revelation.

18. Note here the discussion of the genealogy in D. A. Carson, "Matthew," *The Expositor's Bible Commentary,* vol. 8, ed. Frank E. Gaebelein (Grand Rapids: Zondervan, 1984), 60–70; and Donald A. Hagner, *Matthew,* (Dallas: Word, 1993), 2–12.

19. Donald A. Carson, "Matthew," Frank E. Gaebelein, ed., vol. 8, *Expositor's Bible Commentary,* (Grand Rapids: Zondervan, 1984), 70. In earlier times, letters were used to symbolize numbers, in an interpretive pattern known as "gematria." Hence, any word might also be used to express a numerical value. The Hebrew spelling of David's name adds up to fourteen, as follows: d = 4, v = 6, d = 4; 4 + 6 + 4 = 14 (vowels were not added to the text until later). While gematria is not an exact science, and too much is often made of numbers in Scripture with the result that fantastic interpretations are arrived at, surely Matthew's use of "14" here is meant to draw attention to Jesus' relationship to David and His fulfillment of all that David portended for Israel.

20. The rich theological teaching contained in the genealogy is masterfully detailed by F. D. Bruner, *The Christbook: Matthew 1–12* (Waco: Word, 1987).

21. The language in the text is clear: Mary and Joseph would certainly have had normal sexual union after the birth of Jesus (1:18, 25). The doctrine of Mary's perpetual virginity has no basis in Scripture.

22. This is most likely the explanation as to why Zacharias was struck dumb at his questioning of the angelic messenger (Luke 1:18), and Mary was not when she asked almost the same question of the same angel (Luke 1:34). Zacharias should have recalled the precedent in redemptive history for barren women having had the curse of barrenness removed by God. The wives of the patriarchs, Abraham, Isaac, and Jacob, had all been barren prior to God's gracious intervention, and in the case of Abraham and Sarah, that at their "advanced" age. Samuel, the first prophet in Israel, also was born to a woman previously barren whose womb God "opened." But never before had a virginal conception taken place, and so Mary's question was only to be expected.

23. For example, note the following texts: Genesis 4:5ff., 23–24; 1 Samuel 2:3; Proverbs 6:16; 8:13; 14:3; 16:5; 21:4; Daniel 5:20; Mark 7:20–23; Romans 1:30; 12:3, 16. This is only a partial accounting of what otherwise could be a very long list.

Robert Keith Rapa is professor of Bible at the Moody Bible Institute. He received his Th.D. degree at the University of South Africa while teaching at Asia Baptist Theological Seminary and has degrees from Cornerstone University and Grand Rapids Baptist Seminary, Grand Rapids, Michigan.

4

GOD IN THE FLESH

THE DEITY OF CHRIST

Michael G. Vanlaningham

For more than a decade, two British artists named David Chorley and Douglas Bower waded into the grainfields of England and, using the most rudimentary tools (string, boards, crude sighting devices), formed intriguing geometric patterns in the crops. They did this more than two dozen times each season. The results of their pranks generated a host of explanations, with some suggesting that these crop circles were the result of ball lightning created by atmospheric microwave fields, and others arguing that they had been the landing sites of unidentified flying objects.

The September 23, 1991, issue of *Time* magazine chronicled the actions of the two perpetrators of this giant deception, noting that in response to these unexplained formations, a new science had arose, labeled "cereology," along with a group called "The Circles Effect Research Unit" to study them.[1]

Although the ruse fostered by Chorley and Bower was relatively harmless, deception can also cause great harm. For example, what if the identity of Jesus Christ as the divine Son of God is a fabrication of the early church (as some maintain) and is not true? What if this person had not truly existed, nor had risen from the dead? This would be an ominous hoax indeed.

The doctrine of Christ's deity is one of the foundational truths of the Christian faith. If this belief is nothing more than wishful thinking—or worse, deliberate deception on the part of those who first preached the gospel—then the church's most cherished doctrines cannot stand, and everything else that it has believed about Christ must crumble along with it. Can this ancient truth still be defended today? Does it have any relevance for a sophisticated, technologically driven and theologically uninformed world of the twenty-first century? The starting point in answering these questions is the Old Testament. What does it reveal about the nature of the Messiah?

THE DIVINE MESSIAH

The Son of God

Many critical and even some conservative scholars deny that the Old Testament teaches anything akin to the notion of a divine Messiah. They argue that those passages that Christians have long cited as proof texts for this doctrine were really the result of Semitic exaggeration. They explain that such language was in keeping with the societies of the ancient Middle Eastern world, where their kings were painted in inflated, pseudo-divine terms, without the understanding that they meant anything. But the evidence for such influences from Israel's neighbors is scarce indeed.[2]

However, there are several passages in the Old Testament that offer strong testimony to the divine nature of Israel's promised Messiah.

Many evangelical scholars focus on the concept of the "sonship" of the Messiah in Psalm 2:7 as one of the primary Old Testament proofs of the deity of the Messiah. John F. Walvoord essentially argues that to be a "son of God" means "to be divine."[3] But in the Old Testament, "son of God" was a phrase applied to both angels (Job 1:5–6; 2:1) and to men (Ex. 4:22–23), and Jeremiah 3:19 calls the people of Israel God's sons. Nevertheless, the promises made to David about an anointed son are so extravagant as to take on virtually divine proportions (see 1 Chron. 17:12–14). An implicit question throughout First and Second Chronicles—significantly the last two books in the Hebrew order of the Old Testament—is, "Who is *this* son of David?"

Apparently Solomon thought he might be the fulfillment of this covenant (1 Kings 8:20), but it became obvious that he did not qualify spiritually (see 1 Kings 11:9–12). Nor did Rehoboam qualify. Nor did any other king of Judah in David's line. When one comes to the end of the Hebrew Scriptures, the question on the identity of *the* Davidic son remains unanswered.

Then Matthew begins, "The record of the genealogy of Jesus Christ *the son of David,* the son of Abraham" (Matt. 1:1, emphasis added). Jesus is that Son par excellence.

Psalm 2 asserts the deity of the Messiah in several ways. Charles Hodge has noted that the Messiah is given absolute and universal dominion (2:8–10). He is called Yahweh *(YHWH)* in 2:11, and the psalmist commands the reader to worship Him, something unlikely if the Messiah were a mere mortal. The psalmist urges people to put their trust in this Son and offers motivation for them to do it by offering a blessing to those who do. The consistent witness of the Old Testament is *against* trusting in people and not in God. It is likely, then, that Psalm 2 presents a Messiah who is divine.[4]

God on the Throne

Psalm 45:6–7 is another example in which the psalmist speaks of Israel's Messiah in divine terms.[5] In 45:6, the phrase "Your throne, O God" is the key. While it might be possible to understand 45:6 in the sense "Your throne is divine," or "God is your throne," the traditional understanding is best for several reasons. Both in the verses before and after 45:6, the pronoun "you" predominates, and those uses refer to the king (e.g., 45:2 declares "You are fairer"; "Your lips"; "God has blessed You forever" NASB).[6] When the king is referred to in 45:6 as being upon His throne, He is then called "God," suggesting that this King is divine. Then, in 45:7b, when God is clearly referred to, the psalmist addresses God in the third person, thus distinguishing Him from the (divine) King. In 45:7, the phrase "God, your God," is instructive after the use of "God" in verse 6. While the King may be divine, He must not forget that God is still His God. Implicit here is a distinction between the divine King and the divine God.

One might object that no monotheistic Jewish poet would ever use "God" in the full sense of the word for a king of Israel. But the psalmist could speak of this King's "splendor" and "majesty" (45:3) as well as God's (96:6; the same words are used in both passages); the King's embracing the truth and right (45:4, 6) as well as God's (33:5; 99:4; Isa. 61:8); the King's ability to judge uprightly (45:6b) as well as God's ability (Ps. 67:4; 99:4); and the King's possession of an eternal throne (45:6), similar to God's possession of an eternal throne (10:16; 93:2; 145:13). It does not seem to be as great a disservice to the text as one might think to understand that the King who is extolled in Psalm 45 might be the Davidic King, presented in Psalm 45 as divine.[7]

The King Who Is Lord

Psalm 110 is the most often-quoted Old Testament text in the New Testament. The New Testament writers (and other early

Christian writers) cite it in reference (among other things) to the position of Jesus at the right hand of God (Acts 2:34–35), to the subjection of world powers to Him (1 Cor. 15:25), to Jesus' glory or vindication (Matt. 26:64), and to Jesus' priesthood (Heb. 8:1).[8] For the topic at hand, the question is whether this verse teaches the deity of the Messiah. The main problem comes with the reading offered in the Hebrew text, where the phrase "The LORD says to my Lord" actually contains two distinct words for "Lord." The first, distinguished in the King James Version, New American Standard Bible, and New International Version by small capital letters ("LORD"), translates the Hebrew word *Yahweh*[9] (sometimes transliterated *YHWH*), while the second occurrence of "Lord" is the word *adonai* (literally "my lord"). The difficulty arises with the second term, which, in the form employed in this verse, usually refers to *human* authorities.[10] But *adonai* is probably used in both Joshua 5:14 and Judges 6:13 for *YHWH,* so we can understand the former term in a divine sense here.[11]

Around 200 B.C., Jewish scholars began to translate the Hebrew Scriptures into Greek, then the dominant language in the Mediterranean world. This translation, called the "Septuagint" (sometimes abbreviated "LXX" for the seventy Jewish scholars who, according to tradition, began the translation), gives some indication of what second- and third-century B.C. Jewish scholars thought the Old Testament meant. In Psalm 110:1, they use *kyrios* ("lord") for *both YHWH* and *adonai.* The Septuagint could be rendered something like this: "The Lord God said to my Lord God, 'Sit at My right hand.'" While in the Greek-speaking world, *kyrios* could be used for human masters and leaders, the fact that it is used twice in such close proximity in the Septuagint rendition of the verse, with the first occurrence clearly being a reference to God *(YHWH),* suggests that the Septuagint translators understood *adonai* as a reference to deity.

When one turns to Matthew 22:44–45 and its parallels, it appears that Jesus understood the perspective the religious leaders had on the Messiah to be inadequate. Among the religious experts of early Judaism, the Messiah usually was identified as being the son of David—but no more than this. Jesus queried them on this particular verse and indicated that *His* understanding was that, while the Messiah was not less than the son of David, he was also much more than that. Their understanding was inadequate. Jesus understood Psalm 110:1 to teach a divine Messiah.

Mighty God

In Isaiah 9:6 the prophet states: "For to us a child is born, to us a son is given, and the government will be on his shoulders. And he will be called Wonderful Counselor, Mighty God, Everlasting Father, Prince of Peace."

"Mighty God" *(El Gibbor)* is used frequently for God Himself in the Old Testament, and there seems no good reason not to understand it as a reference to a Son who would also be divine.[12] Isaiah is careful to delineate between God and man, using *El* throughout his book exclusively for God.[13] The case for a divine Messiah is clinched by the presence of the same phrase in Isaiah 10:21: "A remnant will return, a remnant of Jacob will return to the Mighty God *[El Gibbor].*" In Isaiah 10:20, the prophet foretells a time in which those among the faithful remnant of Israel will no longer trust in their earthly allies but in God alone, so that they "will truly rely on the LORD, the Holy One of Israel." The consensus is that this is a reference to God Himself. The parallel with Isaiah 9:6 cannot be overlooked, and it weighs heavily against the purely theophoric understanding of the name —that is, an understanding of the name as being made up of several parts, of which one part is a name or title of God. Furthermore, in Psalm 45:3 (Hebrew, v. 4) *El Gibbor* is used in reference to the Messiah as the "mighty One," and as argued in the discussion on Psalm 45, the Messiah is divine.[14] Arguments against the Messiah being fully divine do not hold up.

JESUS' CLAIM TO BE DIVINE

As we have seen, the doctrine of Christ's deity did not simply appear on the biblical stage without warrant, without precedent.[15] It is a theme found within both the Old Testament and with a number of texts from early Judaism. However, the most important evidence for this doctrine comes from the New Testament. It is here that the deity of Christ is most clearly asserted.

During His later Judean ministry around the time of the Feast of Booths (about six months before His crucifixion), Jesus returned from Galilee to Judea and ministered in and around Jerusalem. This period of ministry was extraordinarily controversial, and one can hardly read through John 7–8 without getting a sense of the intensity of the debates and the almost staccato firing of questions, arguments, and accusations shot at Jesus by His antagonists, as well as His own assertiveness against them. During one dispute centering around the Jewish leaders' pride over their ancestral link to Abraham, Jesus argued that they had more in common with the devil than with the patriarch (John 8:38–41), adding, "Abraham rejoiced [to see] my day" (v. 56 NASB). The Jewish leaders balked at His statement because of Jesus' young age.

Jesus responded, "I tell you the truth . . . before Abraham was born, I am!" (v. 58). Their reaction was to look for stones with which to execute Jesus, most likely for blasphemy.

The crucial issue here is not simply that Jesus claimed preexistence. In early Judaism, some believed in a kind of heavenly preexistence of the Messiah before His appearance on earth. It is more likely that those who heard Christ were offended with the fact that He called Himself by a title that God used for Himself in the Old Testament. The phrase *ego eimi*, meaning "I am" or "I am He," was used nineteen times in Isaiah 40–56 for God's self-assertions.[16] Most of the *ego eimi* assertions by God orbit around the themes of God's eternality (Isa. 41:4; 43:10; 48:12), and His deliverance, restoration, and salvation of Israel (Isa. 43:25; 45:8; 46:4; 48:17; 51:12; 52:6), both themes making an appearance in the context of John 8, with Christ as the center.[17] In John 8:58, then, Jesus was not only claiming preexistence, but He was also claiming to be divine, to be eternal, and to fulfill God's role in delivering His people.[18]

EVIDENCES OF DIVINITY
IN JESUS' EARTHLY MINISTRY

Jesus displayed divine attributes.

Several New Testament narratives suggest Jesus' divine attributes. For example, His actions in the New Testament reveal that He is omnipotent. The divine power of Jesus is seen especially in His effecting of miracles and the statements related to His role in creation. Outside the Gospels, several New Testament books contain statements that assert that Jesus has the power to carry out all things in keeping with His sovereign will. One of these is Ephesians 1:20–23, which emphasizes the exaltation of Christ and the subordination of all earthly and heavenly powers under His feet as a result of the power of God effected through Christ's resurrection. Verse 22 says, "And God placed all things under his feet and appointed him to be head over everything for the church." The fact that God "placed all things under his [Christ's] feet" is coordinated with "appointed him to be head over everything." This absolute authority is one aspect of the omnipotence of Christ.

The New Testament also ascribes to Christ the attribute of omnipresence, i.e., the divine presence everywhere and at the same time. Ephesians 1:22–23 states: "And God placed all things under his feet and appointed him to be head over everything for the church, which is his body, the fullness of him who fills everything in every way." According to these verses, Christ is both omnipotent and omnipresent, filling all things. The meaning of "fill" probably finds its lexical and theological antecedent in the Old Testament verses that speak of the glory of God "filling" the earth or the temple.[19] On the basis of His person and work, then, Jesus Christ is everywhere present, just as God was present in the temple and filling it with His glory.[20]

Another of the attributes of God ascribed to Christ is that of omniscience; like God, Jesus knows all things exhaustively. The divine omniscience of Jesus is seen in a host of ways. The Gospels indicate that Jesus knew what was in the hearts of people (e.g., Matt. 9:4; Mark 2:8) and who would accept and reject Him (John 10:14), and even who would betray Him (John 6:64). But His knowledge extended beyond people to include natural phenomena. Jesus knew that fish would be found and caught in deeper parts of the Sea of Galilee (Luke 5:1–10; John 21:6–11), and that a fish would be caught to provide the necessary funds with which to pay the temple tax (Matt. 17:27).[21] Jesus also claimed knowledge of future events as seen in His outline of prophecy in the Olivet Discourse (Matthew 24–25; Mark 13).

He even had exhaustive foreknowledge of more specific situations, including His betrayal, crucifixion, and resurrection (Luke 9:21) and told His disciples in advance "that when it does happen you will believe" (John 13:19). Thus the omniscient precognition of Jesus serves as one of the foundation stones for validating His identity as the Son of God.

Bruce Ware points out that Jesus predicted precisely the three denials of Peter (John 13:38; 18:19–27), the nature of Peter's death (John 21:18–19), as well as Judas's treachery (John 6:64, 70–71; Matt. 26:21–25). Ware observes, "In all of these cases, Jesus' predictions require that other humans do precisely what Jesus predicted they would do. Yet, these are not presented as mere guesses regarding the future. Rather Jesus *knows* what other free agents will in fact choose to do, [and] *states* what these future actions will be."[22] So the omniscience of Jesus extends even

to the exhaustive knowledge of the future free choices of morally responsible agents (people, demons).

Jesus did what God alone can do.

Many of the passages cited above teach Christ's divinity implicitly. Other passages, which speak of His works, offer explicit evidence of His divine nature. For example, Colossians 1:16
states that Jesus created all things: "For by him all things were
created: things in heaven and on earth, visible and invisible,
whether thrones or powers or rulers or authorities; all things were
created by him and for him" (cf. John 1:3 and Heb. 1:3). If Jesus
Christ is the creator of all things, then He is to be viewed as outside of the created order, all of which implies His deity.

Because He is the Creator, Jesus sustains all that He has created. Paul maintains that in Jesus "all things hold together" (Col.
1:17). The verb "hold together" *(synistemi)* means "continue,
endure, exist, hold together."[23] At the time this was written the
Colossian church was in danger of lapsing back into paganism and
forsaking Christ and Christianity for an influential heresy that had
attracted the church.[24] Paul presented these truths about the Savior to impress upon them His superiority *vis-à-vis* any other religious leader or cult. Why abandon Christ when He is the Creator
and sustainer of all, and the one who has ultimate authority? *What
religion can rival Him?* It was Paul's purpose to present the vast
superiority of Christ to all other rivals for their allegiance in order to motivate them to "stay put" in their ties to Christ.

Jesus' miracles offer additional proof of His deity. They can
be categorized roughly into three kinds: nature miracles, exor-
cisms, and miraculous healings. These miracles served to confirm
Jesus in the messianic role of having great tenderness and mercy
toward the afflicted (e.g., Matt. 14:14; 15:32; 20:34; Mark 1:41),
and of having the obvious stamp of approval from God upon His
ministry.

Jesus exercised divine authority.

We recognize that the miracles by themselves do not necessarily prove the deity of Christ. Other agents in the past performed miracles as well (for example, Moses and Elijah) yet were not divine. However, when the miracles are taken in concert with the other evidences of His divine nature—receiving worship, being the object of prayer, forgiving sins, etc.—they serve to validate His deity. This is especially clear in the healing of the paralytic in Mark 2:3–12 (and parallels in Matt. 9:2–7 and Luke 5:18–25), where Jesus initially offered the man forgiveness of sins. Those standing by rightly recognized that only God could forgive sins (see Isa. 43:25). Jesus then healed the paralytic to prove that He has the authority to forgive sins (Mark 2:10–11). If only God can forgive sins, and if Jesus forgave sins *and proved that He had the authority to do so by healing the paralytic,* then Jesus has divine stature.

Forgiving the sins of people is a prerogative reserved only for God. Christ proved miraculously that He possessed such authority. There were other manifestations of His authority that similarly argued for His deity. For example, Jesus claimed to have the authority to give eternal life. Harris observes that in the Old Testament it was God who was portrayed as the One who provides temporal and eternal salvation (Ps. 62:2, 6; 95:1; Isa. 51:6; Jonah 2:9), and who promises to dispense the blessings of the new covenant (Jer. 31:31–34). But when one turns to the pages of the New Testament, one finds that Jesus Christ is also active as the Deliverer. In Titus, God is called "our Savior" (1:3; 2:10; 3:4) but so is Jesus (1:4; 2:13; 3:6). John says that both God (1 John 5:11) and Jesus grant eternal life (John 10:28; 17:2). The apostle Paul states that God has "rescued us from the dominion of darkness" through Christ and that Jesus will deliver believers from "the coming wrath" (Col. 1:13; 1 Thess. 1:10). Hebrews 5:9 announces that Jesus is "the source of eternal salvation." And in many of the greetings in Paul's epistles, he makes both God and Jesus the source of grace and peace (for example, Rom. 1:7; 1 Cor. 1:3).[25]

The authority to execute all judgment is another aspect of divine authority. The Old Testament clearly ascribes to God the judgment of the world (Ps. 9:7–8; 96:10–13). But when one turns to the New Testament, it is Jesus Christ who is entrusted by God with the task of judgment (John 5:22, 27; see Acts 10:42). Paul declared, "In the past God overlooked such ignorance, but now he commands all people everywhere to repent. For he has set a day when he will judge the world with justice by the man he has appointed" (Acts 17:30–31). Jesus declared that He will sit on His glorious throne and judge the sheep and the goats (righteous and unrighteous) following His second coming to determine who will enter the kingdom of God (Matt. 25:31–46). Paul says that every believer will stand before the judgment seat of God (Rom. 14:10) and before the judgment seat of Christ (2 Cor. 5:10) to give an account of his life; this suggests that the evaluating of the believer will be carried out by God through Christ. Surely one who judges in this manner must be able to read the hearts of all people; so the omniscience, authority, and omnipotence of Christ prepare Him to rightly judge.

JESUS IS THE IMAGE OF GOD

Christ's attributes, works, and authority all reveal that a marked correlation exists between the person and work of God in the Old Testament and the person and work of Jesus in the New Testament. Further, the apostle Paul has applied to Jesus several Old Testament passages that highlight God's work and authority. The prophet Joel wrote, "And everyone who calls on the name of the LORD will be saved; for on Mount Zion and in Jerusalem there will be deliverance, as the LORD has said, among the survivors whom the LORD calls." Here "the LORD" is clearly a reference to *YHWH* God (2:32). In Romans 10:13, however, Paul cites the Old Testament verse in reference to *Jesus*, making Him the source of deliverance for the people of God. Similarly, Isaiah wrote, "'The Redeemer will come to Zion, to those in Jacob who repent of their sins,' declares the LORD" (59:20). The context indicates that the Redeemer is none other than God Himself, but in Romans 11:26, Paul applies it to Christ.

The Alpha and the Omega

Other New Testament writers have the same focus, including the apostle John and the writer of Hebrews. In Isaiah 44:6, the prophet writes, "This is what the LORD says—Israel's King and Redeemer, the LORD Almighty: I am the first and I am the last; apart from me there is no God." The same statement about God being first and last is recorded in two other places in Isaiah as well (Isa. 41:4; 48:12). In Revelation, John does much the same thing: He records the vision in which Jesus Christ calls Himself "the first and the last" three times (Rev. 1:17; 2:8; 22:13). He notes that Jesus also calls Himself "the Alpha and the Omega . . . who is, and who was, and who is to come, the Almighty" (1:8). Concerning these references, G. K. Beale asserts,

> The expressions [in Isaiah and in Rev 1:8 in which God says "I am the alpha and omega"] refer to God's sovereignty over history, especially in fulfillment of prophecy and in bringing world affairs to a climax in salvation and judgment. God is transcendent over time and governs the way history proceeds because he is in control of its inception and conclusion. What was said of God in Isaiah and in Rev. 1:8 is now applied to Christ. . . . He possesses the same transcendent attribute as God. This transferal is elucidated in 22:13 in such a way that Christ there (and here) must be understood as a divine figure. As in Isaiah, the expression functions in v 17b to assure

John and his readers that Christ is in control of the vicissi-
tudes of history, however bad they seem. Indeed, he is the
force behind history, causing it to fulfill his purposes.[26]

These parallels indicate an identity in nature (though a distinction in the Persons must be maintained) that is shared by God
the Father and God the Son, serving as another support for the
deity of Christ.[27]

The Embodiment of God

In three other texts Jesus is said to be the very embodiment
of God. According to Colossians 1:15, Jesus is "the image of the
invisible God." The word *image* comes from the Greek word
eikon, from which is derived the English term *icon,* an image of
a person or saint. In the first-century Greek-speaking world,
eikon was used for the copy or image of something, such as a
painting, a statue, or the figure of a person on a coin. The image was thought to share in the reality of the thing or person
represented.[28] When Jesus Christ is called the "image of God,"
the emphasis is upon the equality of the image with the original.
In support of this is the fact that Jesus is said to be "in the form
of God" and "equal with God" (Phil. 2:6). Jesus Himself declared
that to see Him is to see God (John 12:45; 14:9). It would be
impossible for Jesus to be the precise image of God if He Himself were not fully divine.

Finally, Colossians 2:9 declares, "For in Christ all the fullness
of the Deity lives in bodily form." This "fullness," from the Greek
pleroma (used also in Col. 1:19 as God's "fullness dwell[ing] in
[the Son]"), is defined further by the phrase "of the Deity," probably referring to the divine essence of God—the very being of
God. So in Jesus Christ one finds a Person who is of the divine
nature. The expression "all the fullness" is a redundancy arguing
for the fullness of the divine essence residing in Christ *alone* (in

116

bodily form; the same divine essence is possessed by the other members of the Trinity as well).[29] "Bodily form" (*somatikos*, as in "psycho*somatic*") is to be understood as a reference to Christ in His incarnation, resurrection, and ascension. While He possessed the divine essence before the Incarnation, He did not possess them *in bodily form*. But now, in His glorified, resurrected body, Jesus possesses full deity, so that He *still* has the fullness of deity in bodily form.[30] If the Colossian heretics who were influencing the true church thought they had something wonderful in their system of belief, the Christians in Colossae had *Jesus Christ!*

The Radiance of God's Glory

Finally, in Hebrews 1:3, we read, "The Son is the radiance of God's glory and the exact representation of his being." The phrase "exact representation" comes from the Greek *charakter,* meaning our "character." In classical Greek (preceding the Septuagint and New Testament), the phrase was used to describe the embossing or stamping of a figure onto a coin, other metal, or wood and came to refer to one's unique and unalterable physical and mental qualities. Used in this verse, it refers to Jesus Christ as having "the impress of God's nature" upon Him. He is the one on whom God has stamped "His nature," which includes the "radiance of His glory."[31] William Lane states, "In v. 3a he [the writer of Hebrews] used the word [*charakter,* 'exact representation'] to convey as emphatically as he could his conviction that in Jesus Christ there had been provided a perfect, visible expression of the reality [better 'essence' or 'nature'] of God."[32]

The purpose of Hebrews is much the same as that of Colossians. Apparently there were some among this Christian assembly (consisting of Jewish believers primarily) who were in the process of forsaking Christianity and reverting to Judaism. The writer of the book urges them to press on all the way to "perfection," to the perfect new covenant, the superior priesthood, to which the Old Testament (especially the things stipulated in the Law of Moses) versions were only mere shadows.

JESUS IS CALLED "GOD"

John 1

One of the stronger arguments in support of the deity of Christ is found in the New Testament writers' tendency to ascribe to Him the title *Theos,* meaning "God." John 1:1 makes three statements, each about the Word (who is Christ, according to v. 17). The first is that the Word (Greek, *Logos*) existed ("was") in the beginning, a phrase that implies His existing before creation. The second is that He enjoyed fellowship "with God," supporting the idea that the Word is distinct from God the Father.[33] The third proposition indicates that the Word was divine but does not allow for the possibility that He was ever "elevated to divine status." Murray J. Harris writes, "The thought of the verse moves from eternal preexistence to personal intercommunion [between the Logos and God] to intrinsic deity."[34] Only because the Logos was divine can it be said of Him that He existed before creation occurred and had unbroken association with the Father.

In John 1:18 Jesus is described as "God the One and Only" who has "made him [God] known." Although some versions (notably the KJV and NASB) use the phrase "only begotten" to translate the adjective that the NIV renders "the One and Only," this is probably not a particularly good translation of the word *monogenes*. It is often understood from its constituent parts to mean "only" or "alone" *(mono)* "born" *(gennao,* "to beget, give birth to"), so that Jesus is viewed as the only one created by God, and who then created everything else for God.[35] But the word is more likely a combination of *mono* and the word *genos,* which can

118

mean "kind" or "sort."[36] If this is the case, then this verse, and the others that use "only begotten" in reference to Christ,[37] say nothing of the concept of Him being created by God but instead refer to His unique status as literally "one of a kind." "Only begotten" is used in the sense of "unique" in Hebrews 11:17, where Isaac is called Abraham's "only begotten son." Isaac was not Abraham's only son; Ishmael preceded him, and Abraham had other sons with Keturah (Gen. 25:4). In four of the eight occurrences of *monogenes* in the New Testament, it describes "Son." In three other occurrences, it is used alone as a noun, but the context makes it clear that it means "only son" (John 1:14; Heb. 11:17), "only child" (Luke 9:38), or "only daughter" (Luke 8:42). Since the word typically describes familial relations, the best way to translate the phrase in John 1:18 is, "the special (unique, one of a kind) Son, who is God, has explained Him."[38] This verse cannot be pressed to mean that Jesus is "the only one created by God who is a god."

Thomas's Declaration

The words uttered by Thomas when he first saw Christ following the Resurrection provide another example where Christ is referred to as "God" (John 20:28). It is unlikely that Thomas's reference to Jesus as "my God" equates Jesus with God the Father, since Jesus differentiated Himself from the Father in John 20:17. It would also be incorrect to see in the term "God" the diluted sense that God was only active in Jesus in a remarkable way. Harris says, "As used by a monotheistic Jew in reference to a person who was demonstrably human, . . . [*Theos*, "God"] will denote oneness with the Father in being (cf. John 10:30), not merely in purpose and action. In other words, Thomas's cry expresses the substantial divinity of Jesus."[39]

Other New Testament Passages

A number of points support the idea that the "God over all" mentioned in Romans 9:5 is none other than Jesus Christ. More than likely, the phrase "who is" in this verse has its nearest and most reasonable antecedent in "Christ," since they share case, number, and gender. The contrasting phrases "the human ancestry of Christ" and "God over all" should be understood as complementary, emphasizing both the incarnational and divine aspects of Christ's person.

In Titus 2:13 Paul refers to the "blessed hope" as "the glorious appearing of our great God and Savior, Jesus Christ." A similar phrase appears in 2 Peter 1:1, where the apostle speaks of "the righteousness of our God and Savior Jesus Christ." The phrase probably does not refer to God the Father and to Jesus Christ as two persons. The expression "God and Savior" was used often in the first century in diverse religious settings and was used as a label for God among the Jewish people. In those cases, the phrase denoted one deity, not two. Furthermore, the grammatical construction of the phrase also suggests that only one person is being referred to, not two.[40] "God" is further defined and expanded by the word "Savior" but not distinguished from it. Thus the sense is, ". . . the glory of our great God, who is the Savior, and that is Jesus Christ."[41]

We should note further that Jesus accepted worship from people and angels freely (Matt. 14:33; Heb. 1:6). The Scriptures make it clear that mere mortals or angels are not to be worshiped (Matt. 4:10; Acts 10:25–26; 14:11–13; Rev. 19:10). He also instructed His followers to offer prayer in His name (John 16:24). Both actions indicate that Jesus saw Himself as the divine Son of God. He delegated authority and power to the Twelve so that they could preach, heal, and raise the dead (Matt. 10:1, 7–8). All this suggests that He is much more than a great human. He is the divine Son of God, the second member of the Godhead.

EARLY CHURCH DISPUTES
REGARDING THE DEITY OF CHRIST

The deity of Christ raises extremely important questions for which some in the early church had differing and aberrant answers. How does one guard the Old Testament bastion of monotheism and accept the deity of Jesus? How can God be said to reside in human flesh? Forming answers to these questions posed an enormous challenge to the early church.

Ebionite Heresy

One group, called the Ebionites, apparently originated following the destruction of Jerusalem in A.D. 70. They kept the Law of Moses ruthlessly, venerated Jerusalem, and preferred the Gospel of Matthew and the epistle of James to anything in the "anti-Semitic" letters of Paul. They taught that God was one, based on emphasis, and that Jesus was not divine in the sense outlined especially in the fourth Gospel. Jesus was the Messiah, but in the sense emphasized in most of early Judaism, namely, that He was human and that He was not virgin born. But at His baptism, the power and influence of God—the Christ—came upon Jesus, partly due to Jesus' fidelity to the Law. He served with this power from God, functioning something like a prophet, but "the Christ" departed from Him prior to His crucifixion.

Ebionite doctrine sacrificed the equality of Jesus Christ with God the Father on the altar of monotheism. Jesus received exalted—but not divine—status for the Son. As a result, the early church fathers unanimously and rightly condemned the heresy. Much of liberal Protestant and Roman Catholic Christology, as well as certain beliefs of traditional Mormonism, bears a considerable resemblance to Ebionite Christology.

Arian Heresy

A second dispute arose around a group that received its direction from a North African priest named Arius (A.D. 256–336), born probably in Libya. After Arius was condemned by both a local council convened by Bishop Alexander and a synod in Antioch, Emperor Constantine was concerned enough about the heat the controversy was generating in his realm that he assembled what is called the first ecumenical council, the Council of Nicea (modern Isnik, Turkey).

Arius taught that God was an absolutely transcendent being, unchanging in His existence (immutable), and that no one could share in His divine nature. Hence, Jesus could not be divine in the same sense that the Father was divine for, among other things, Christ is said to have grown and matured. Arius also taught that the relationship of human fathers and sons was analogous to the relationship of God and Jesus. Since human fathers precede their sons, so God existed before Christ and created Him before all other creatures. There was therefore a time when Jesus did not exist. Such terms as "only begotten" and "firstborn," considered previously, were thought by Arius to substantiate this position.

The Council of Nicea formulated a statement that served to condemn Arius and his followers and to clarify orthodox belief. As noted in chapter 1, this Nicene Creed identified Jesus Christ as "the Son of God, . . . true God of true God, begotten not made, one in being with the father, through whom all things came to be."

Despite the decision and statement of the council, the issue was not resolved immediately nor was a consensus reached. But in the end, Bishop Athanasius prevailed, assisted by three others—Gregory of Nyssa, Basil the Great, and Gregory of Nazianzus. Arian beliefs continue today in some forms of Unitarianism, and especially in the dogmas of the Jehovah's Witnesses.[42]

A FEW CONTEMPORARY VIEWS
OF THE DEITY OF CHRIST

A fair amount of New Testament scholarship today denies that much, if anything, can be known about Jesus. Many see Him as an invention of the early church, so that who He was cannot be known without looking through the veil of the early church's "creativity."[43] But if Jesus is an invention of the early church, one must ask, "Who invented the early church?"

Among those who are more optimistic about the knowledge of Christ in the Gospels, there has been a tendency to focus upon Christology "from below," emphasizing the humanity and the earthly ministry of Christ. The propensity is to see Jesus as divine only from the standpoint that He functions as God's agent on earth, or that He reveals God, and in that sense is "divine."[44] But this is a serious redefinition of the "deity" of Christ in comparison to the New Testament teaching, and the Gospel According to John makes it clear that it is precisely because Jesus is divine that He is able to act as the revealer of God and as His agent (John 1:18). Any Christology that fails to take this into account has not done justice to the contents of the New Testament.

WHY THE DEITY OF CHRIST MATTERS

What if Jesus Christ were not fully divine? Could He still be the Savior of the world? Down through the centuries, orthodox Christian scholars have responded to these questions with an emphatic "No!" There are several reasons why the doctrine of the deity of Christ is of practical importance to the church. First, only one who was divine could satisfactorily explain the Divine One to man. The apostle John wrote, "No one has ever seen God, but God the One and Only, who is at the Father's side, has made him known" (John 1:18). Jesus' ability to reveal God to us is predicated upon His being divine.

Second, only one who is divine could resurrect Christ. If Jesus were only human, it would not be possible for Him to resurrect Himself. How could a mortal raise himself from the dead? Yet John 2:19–21 indicates that He anticipated raising Himself. Without the divine nature, He could not have done this.

Third, only God in the flesh could serve as the mediator between God and man. It is difficult to imagine a mere creature being able to bridge the gap between sinners and God. Would it be possible for a finite creature to effect the eternal salvation of people or turn away the eternal wrath of God? Surely these things require a divine Redeemer!

Fourth, if Jesus is not in possession of all the attributes of deity, then Christians have been involved either in polytheism or idolatry since the inception of the faith.

Fifth, if Jesus is not the second member of the Godhead, then the Scriptures are either involved in a great deception or in a serious error. In either case they cannot and should not be trusted.

Finally, as one examines the contexts of the great statements about the deity of Christ, a dual apologetic and exhortative purpose seem to dominate. Jesus is presented as the one who "fills all" in Ephesians, indicating that the powers that were so rampant in Ephesus and the Roman world as a whole could not compete with Him. This would serve to steady the believers there. In Colossians, a heresy was becoming attractive to the believers; but Paul emphasizes the superiority of Christ to all other rivals, so that abandoning Him becomes unthinkable. The great Christological statements in the fourth Gospel were written to convince people that Jesus, who is the Messiah, is also the divine Son of God, so that John's readers would place their faith in Him if they had not already done so. The writer of Hebrews extols the superiority of Christ to anything in Judaism, urging his readers to cleave to Jesus.

Thus the deity of Christ in the Bible serves to engender faith *and perseverance in that faith* in the face of challenges to the contrary.

NOTES

1. "It Happens in the Best Circles," *Time*, 23 September 1991, 59; cited in Murray J. Harris, *Three Crucial Questions About Jesus* (Grand Rapids: Baker, 1994), 13, 111.
2. For this opinion, see B. B. Warfield, "The Divine Messiah in the Old Testament," *Biblical and Theological Studies* (reprint, Philadelphia: Presbyterian & Reformed, 1968), 96–100 and the literature cited there.
3. John F. Walvoord, *Jesus Christ Our Lord* (Chicago: Moody, 1969), 41–42. See also Charles Hodge, *Systematic Theology*, vol. 1 (reprint, Grand Rapids: Eerdmans, 1982), 491.
4. Hodge, *Systematic Theology*, 491.
5. The following discussion of Psalm 45 summarizes the superb work of Murray J. Harris, *Jesus As God: The New Testament Use of* Theos *in Reference to Jesus* (Grand Rapids: Baker, 1992), 187–204.
6. In 45:3–5, one finds "Your sword," "Your splendor . . . majesty . . . right hand . . . arrows." Similarly in 45:8 appears "Your garments."
7. Hebrews 1:8–9 quotes the Septuagint version of Ps. 45:6–7. The treatment of the psalm will have to serve double duty as treatment for the use of it in Hebrews. On *theos* in Heb. 1:7–8, cf. Harris, *Jesus As God,* 205–27.
8. This summary is drawn from W. D. Davies and Dale C. Allison Jr., *A Critical and Exegetical Commentary on the Gospel According to Saint Matthew: Matthew 19–28* , *International Critical Commentary,* ed. J.A. Emerton, vol. 3 (Edinburgh: T & T Clark, 1997), 3:253.
9. In this study, all Hebrew words are shown in transliterated form for the convenience of the non-Hebrew reader.
10. Herbert W. Bateman IV, "Psalm 110:1 and the New Testament," *Bibliotheca Sacra* 149 (October–December 1992): 448.
11. Barry C. Davis, "Is Psalm 110 a Messianic Psalm?" *Bibiotheca Sacra* 157 (April–June 2000): 162–63.
12. See the use of *El Gibbor* in Deut. 10:17; Neh. 9:32; Ps. 24:8; Jer. 23:18.
13. See, e.g., Isa. 31:3: "Now the Egyptians are men *[adam]*, and not God *[El]*, and their horses are flesh and not spirit." In Isa. 7:14, the name of the Messiah, *Immanuel*, indicates that God is present with *man*. For this argument, see E. J. Young, *The Book of Isaiah*, vol. 1 (Grand Rapids: Eerdmans, 1965), 336. The term *elohim*, usually translated "God," is (rarely) used for people in the Old Testament (see Ex. 22:8–9, "judges"; Ps. 82:1, "rulers"), but *el* never is. This makes it unlikely that *El Gibbor* refers to a mere man infused with the special power of God, or a purely human ruler who becomes deified by the people of Israel. This is the more remarkable because *El Gibbor* is said to be a "child born to us," a phrase that suggests the humanity of this Mighty God.
14. So says Robert L. Reymond, *Jesus, Divine Messiah: The Old Testament Witness* (Rossshire, Scotland: Christian Focus, 1990), 50–51.
15. Similarly J. L. Houlden, *Jesus: A Question of Identity* (London: SPCK, 1992), 62–66.
16. Isaiah 43:10, 25 (twice); 45:8, 18, 19 (twice), 22; 46:4 (twice), 9; 47:12 (twice); 48:12 (twice), 17; 51:12 (twice); 52:6. In Isa. 46:9–10a (NASB), God says, "Remember the former things long past, for I am God, and there is no other; I am God, and there is no one like Me, declaring the end from the beginning. . . ." Here God claims a uniqueness for Himself that is shared with no one. Yet Jesus calls Himself by the same appellation and claims to fulfill the role of salvation which

God said He would fulfill. It is understandable why those who heard Jesus would seek to stone Him for blasphemy.

17. In John 8:24 (NASB), Jesus uses the "I am [He]" expression in relation to deliverance being found only in Him. See also 8:32–36, 51; for His eternality, see 8:42, 56, 58.

18. For other verses on the eternality of Jesus Christ, see John 1:1; 12:41; 17:5; 1 Cor. 10:4; Phil. 2:6; Heb. 11:26; 13:8; Jude 5.

19. Ezekiel 43:5; 44:4; Isa. 6:1; Jer. 23:24; Hag. 2:7. For these references and the point drawn from them, see Peter T. O'Brien, *The Letter to the Ephesians* (Grand Rapids: Eerdmans, 1999), 149.

20. Other verses that support the omnipresence of Christ include Matt. 18:20; 28:20; Rom. 8:9; Gal. 2:20; Eph. 3:17; Col. 1:27; and Rev. 3:20.

21. These points are drawn from Thomas Schultz, "The Doctrine of the Person of Christ with an Emphasis upon the Hypostatic Union" (Th.D. diss., Dallas Theological Seminary, 1962), 194–95; cited in Josh McDowell and Bart Larson, *Jesus: A Biblical Defense of His Deity* (San Bernardino, Calif.: Here's Life, 1983), 53–54.

22. Bruce A. Ware, *God's Lesser Glory: The Diminished God of Open Theism* (Wheaton, Ill.: Crossway, 2000), 127; italics in the original.

23. Walter Bauer, Frederick William Danker, W. F. Arndt, and F. W. Gingerich, *A Greek-English Lexicon of the New Testament,* 3d ed. (Chicago: Univ. of Chicago: 2000), 97.

24. Representative of this understanding of the purpose of the book is Murray J. Harris, *Colossians and Philemon* (Grand Rapids: Eerdmans, 1991), 5.

25. Harris, *Three Crucial Questions,* 86.

26. G. K. Beale, *The Book of Revelation: A Commentary on the Greek Text* (Grand Rapids: Eerdmans, 1999), 213.

27. For numerous other examples, see Harris, *Three Crucial Questions,* 88–92.

28. O. Flender, "Image—*[eikon],*" *New International Dictionary of New Testament Theology,* ed. Colin Brown, vol. 2 (Grand Rapids: Zondervan, 1976), 286–87.

29. "Fullness" is already a superlative term, and to describe it as "*all* fullness" is a bit like saying, "Michael Jordan is an *amazingly awesome* athlete."

30. For these and other points, see Harris, *Colossians and Philemon,* 98–99.

31. J. Gess, "Image—*[charakter],*" *New International Dictionary of New Testament Theology,* ed. Colin Brown, vol. 2 (Grand Rapids: Zondervan, 1976), 288–89.

32. William Lane, *Hebrews,* vol. 47, *Word Bible Commentary* (Dallas: Word, 1991), 13.

33. This fact weighs heavily against the view held by the United Pentecostal Church and other "Jesus only" movements, which maintain that Jesus equals God *not only in essence but in person,* so that the doctrine of the Trinity is effectively denied. If Jesus, the Word, was *with* God the Father, then He cannot be identical with Him. Thus there is a plurality in the Godhead.

34. Harris, *Jesus As God,* 71.

35. It is dangerous to define compound words from their individual parts when studying the Bible in the original languages. In English, for example, one cannot get a sense of what "butterfly" means by examining the words "butter" and "fly." The same can be said for "pineapple," or my favorite, "Grapenuts," which are made of wheat and barley, among other things, but contain neither grapes nor nuts.

36. Bauer et al., *A Greek-English Lexicon,* 156.

37. John 1:14, 18; 3:16, 18; 1 John 4:9.

38. See Harris, *Jesus As God,* 84–92. I have modified his views slightly. If I read him correctly, he would apparently object to the way I define "only begotten" to mean "unique, special, one-of-a-kind." Otherwise, the points above are his.

39. Harris, *Jesus As God*, 125.
40. Specifically, there are two nouns in the same case ("God" and "Savior") that are governed by one article (which is not translatable) that is also in the same case as the nouns. These nouns are connected with a conjunction ("and"). For the same construction, see 2 Cor 1:3, where the phrase "the God and Father . . ." indicates that one person is described with two terms.
41. Harris, *Jesus As God*, 178–82.
42. For a good summary of Arianism and the Council of Nicea, see Louis Berkhof, *The History of Christian Doctrines* (Grand Rapids: Baker, 1937), 83–90.
43. This was one of the assumptions of the Jesus Seminar and is an approach that finds its strongest support in the writings of Robert Funk and Marcus Borg, among others.
44. For example, Karl Barth, *Church Dogmatics* (Edinburgh: T & T Clark, 1960) (which is a work in four "volumes," but most of the volumes have multiple sections or whole books, hence "1.2" means "volume one, book two"), 4.2 (1958) 105–9; 1.2 (1956) 167–88; 4.1 (1956) 35; 4.3.1 (1961) 409.

Michael G. Vanlaningham is professor of Bible at the Moody Bible Institute. He earned his Ph.D. from Trinity Evangelical Divinity School and also has academic degrees from Nebraska Wesleyan University in Lincoln, Nebraska, and Talbot Theological Seminary in La Mirada, California. He has served as a pastor for seventeen years.

5

NOTHING BUT THE BLOOD

THE SUBSTITUTIONARY ATONEMENT OF CHRIST

Gregg Quiggle

One of my vivid memories as a child attending church is of congregational singing. I remember standing by my parents and glancing up at their faces as we sang together. I recall their earnest joy as, surrounded by friends and neighbors, we belted out each verse. Robert Lowry's hymn "Nothing but the Blood" was a particular favorite of our little Baptist congregation. Its haunting questions, followed by the bold proclamation of the chorus concerning the power of Christ's blood, seemed to reverberate off the roof and walls of our little sanctuary.

The words and the music made a striking impression on my young heart and mind:

What can wash away my sins? Nothing but the blood of Jesus;
What can make me whole again? Nothing but the blood
   of Jesus.
Oh precious is the flow, that makes me white as snow;
No other fount I know, Nothing but the blood of Jesus.[1]

Now that I am an adult I find myself not only fondly recalling the experience of singing that hymn but also thinking about the importance of the words. One of the core assertions of historic Christianity is the belief that Christ's death makes human salvation possible. Theologically, this involves the work of Jesus Christ, God incarnate. What was, and is, the meaning of Christ's death on the cross? How has the church understood Christ's death, and why is it important to those of us who claim to follow Christ in the twenty-first century?

OUR NEED FOR ATONEMENT

The word *atonement* carries in it the idea of reconciliation—literally a bringing together, or an *at–one–ment*. In a sense, this was the "mission statement" for Christ's life on earth. As the apostle Paul put it, "God was reconciling the world to himself in Christ, not counting men's sins against them" (2 Cor. 5:19). This involved more for Christ than simply becoming one of us. Merely "visiting" His estranged creatures was not enough. In fact, the culmination of His time on earth—His death, burial, and resurrection—comprise the very heart of the gospel itself (1 Cor. 15:3–4). In short, Christ's work was to make possible, by His life, death, and resurrection, reconciliation between a sinful, rebellious humanity and a holy, righteous God.

The Bible is very clear that this was a work that only Jesus could accomplish. The Scripture declares that "it is impossible for the blood of bulls and goats to take away sins" (Heb. 10:4). Indeed, Jesus came to "give his life as a ransom for many" (Mark

10:45). Romans 5 affirms that it is through the person and work of Christ that humans are redeemed. When the Philippian jailer asked Paul what he must do to be saved, the apostle replied: "Believe in the Lord Jesus" (Acts 16:31).

We cannot make ourselves acceptable to God. Christ alone makes salvation possible. Christianity is not a "self-help" theory, or a "do-it-yourself" religion. To make such claims would be to make a mockery of Christ's death. If we could reconcile ourselves to God by our own effort, apart from Christ's death, it would, at best, make His death a mere moral example, or, at worst, make it superfluous.

However, if the core concept behind the biblical doctrine of atonement is reconciliation, it also necessarily presupposes that there has been estrangement. Those who are being reconciled were once alienated from Him. The source of the estrangement is something the theologians refer to as "original sin," and its effect has been described as "total depravity."

Original sin refers to the sinful condition all human beings have inherited from their ancestor Adam (Rom. 5:12). The Bible teaches that all the wreckage we see in our lives, and the lives of others, had its origin in the sin of Adam and Eve. Genesis 3 provides a narrative of this tragedy, wherein Adam and Eve bring destruction on themselves. They both disobeyed God by eating fruit from the Tree of the Knowledge of Good and Evil. Romans explains that by this one act sin and death entered, not only into Adam and Eve but all their descendants as well (5:12). This act even enslaved the whole of creation (8:20–21). The apostle Paul asserts we were all in Adam, and thus there is solidarity with Adam that links us to this original sin (Rom. 5:12–21 and 2 Cor. 5:22).

The consequences of this original sin were devastating and all-encompassing. Because of Adam's role as our representative, his disobedience changed our relationship to God. It also changed human nature. As a result of Adam's disobedience, I am fallen and sinful, "sold as a slave to sin" (Rom. 7:14). It is important to recognize, however, that total depravity is a qualitative, not a quantitative, statement. It asserts that every part of our being has been affected by Adam's sin, not that we are all as sinful as possible. We can see manifestations of sin to varying degrees in our lives. That is why, to some extent, the consequences of slavery to sin are unique in each person, while the slavery itself is universal. For example, some people are addicted to food, while others are addicted to gossip. Some people have bad knees while others have bad eyes. What is universal is the fact that we all are marked and captive to sin.

The proof of this universal human plight is clear and compelling—death itself. There is something profoundly wrong with all of us. Every one of us is a "dead man walking" and there is nothing we can do to stave off our own mortality.

Total depravity also means we are locked in rebellion against God, under the power of sin, spiritually dead and guilty (Rom. 1–3; 6–7). In short, helpless and thus hopeless, we live as bound sinners, enemies of God, facing His just condemnation.

Clearly, the human race was in desperate need of atonement. Thankfully, God acted by initiating reconciliation with us. As the apostle Paul put it in Romans 5:8, 10, "But God demonstrates his own love for us in this: While we were still sinners, Christ died for us" so that, "when we were God's enemies, we were reconciled to him through the death of his Son."

ASPECTS OF THE ATONEMENT

Triumph and Sacrifice

Although *atonement* refers primarily to the concept of reconciliation, there are a number of additional ideas associated with it in Scripture. One of these is the theme of triumph. In Colossians 2:8–15, Paul exhorted the church to stand firm against false teaching and the surrounding paganism and based his appeal on the triumph of Christ. In these verses Paul reminded the Colossian believers that Christ, by His death, burial, and resurrection, had already triumphed over the things that threatened them. He "disarmed the powers and authorities" and "made a public spectacle of them, triumphing over them by the cross" (Col. 2:15).

The triumph of Christ through His atoning work is also an important theme in the book of Revelation. In Revelation 5, for example, Christ is called "the Lion of the tribe of Judah," but is pictured as a lamb that has been slain (5–6). He alone is declared to be worthy to open the scroll that signals that outpouring of divine judgment, with this explanation: "because you were slain, and with your blood you purchased men for God from every tribe and language" (v. 9). It is Christ's death that gives Him the authority to do what no mere creature could do. By virtue of His death, the redeemed and the angels together proclaim, "Worthy is the Lamb, who was slain, to receive power and wealth and wisdom and strength and honor and glory and praise!" (v. 12). Clearly part of the atoning work of Christ is His triumph over all things.[2]

The biblical concept of atonement is also linked to sacrifice. *Sacrifice* is a term used extensively in the Old Testament, particularly in the context of our relationship to God. The extensive sacrificial system laid out in the Old Testament shows the seriousness of sin and hints at what would be necessary for its removal. Perhaps one of the best examples is found in Leviticus 4:13–20, where instructions are given for sacrifices to be made on behalf of the congregation of Israel. This passage shows the seriousness of sin from God's perspective, especially in view of the provision it makes for dealing with unintentional sins of which the community is initially unaware. This is hardly, from a human point of view, a major offense; yet, the text indicates atonement and forgiveness are necessary. The seriousness of sin is further reinforced by the fact that death and the shedding of blood were necessary for atonement. A sacrifice had to be made if Israel was to be forgiven, even when the sin was unintentional.

These and similar Old Testament texts provide the context for the New Testament's description of Christ's death as "sacrificial." Matthew seemed to be alluding to this when he recorded Christ's statement, "This is my blood of the covenant, which is poured out for many for the forgiveness of sins" (Matt. 26:28). The writer of the book of Hebrews was even more explicit, arguing Christ not only fulfilled the office of high priest but completed the sacrificial system as well (Hebrews 9–10). Again and again Hebrews shows how Christ's sacrifice did what the old system of sacrifice could never fully accomplish, the removal and forgiveness of sins. In the Old Testament, Israel's relationship with God was provisionally secured by a heartfelt obedience to the sacrificial system. According to the New Testament, Christ's sacrificial atoning work on the cross secures a binding reconciliation with God for the believing sinner.

Expiation and Propitiation

Expiation and *propitiation* are two other important terms linked to the notion of atonement. Together they flesh out all that is involved in the idea of forgiveness of sins. They reveal the means whereby our guilt is removed. If we are to be at one with God, a cleansing and a turning away of God's wrath is necessary. Expiation has to do with the notion of cleaning up or removing defilement and the cancellation of sin. Propitiation denotes the turning away of God's wrath. There are two distinct, yet inseparable issues. One has to do with us as humans. Specifically, how are we forgiven? This is the question of expiation. The second has to do with God. Specifically, how is God's wrath appeased, or assuaged? This is the question of propitiation.

In many modern translations, the word *expiation* is not used. It is simply translated "atonement." However, the New American Standard version uses it in Numbers 35:33, and the meaning of the term is apparent: "So you shall not pollute the land in which you are; for blood pollutes the land and no expiation can be made for the land for the blood that is shed on it, except by the blood of him who shed it." We see here the idea of cleansing. As with propitiation, the shedding of blood is a critical component of this process.

Propitiation is also not widely used in the Bible. In John's first epistle, the idea of propitiation appears twice. John wrote: "My dear children, I write this to you so that you will not sin. But if anybody does sin, we have one who speaks to the Father in our defense—Jesus Christ, the Righteous One. He is the atoning sacrifice [literally, the propitiation] for our sins, and not only for ours but also for the sins of the whole world" (1 John 2:1–2). Later John added, "This is love: not that we loved God, but that he loved us and sent his Son as an atoning sacrifice [propitiation] for our sins" (4:10). In both cases Jesus is identified as the one who serves to propitiate.

Hebrews ties Christ's propitiatory act directly to the Old Testament: "For this reason [Christ] had to be made like his brothers in every way, in order that he might become a merciful and faithful high priest in service to God, and that he might make atonement for the sins of the people" (2:17). Leviticus 16 provides the backdrop for this. On the Day of Atonement, "Yom Kippur," the high priest selected two goats and cast lots between them. One became the sacrificial goat and the other the scapegoat. The sacrificial goat was slaughtered, and the high priest spread its blood on the lid or atonement cover of the ark of the covenant. The purpose of this was to propitiate God's wrath incurred because of Israel's sin. By this act, God's wrath toward Israel was assuaged. The high priest then took the other goat, the so-called scapegoat, and symbolically placed his hands on it and confessed the sins of Israel over it. The goat was taken out of the camp and released into the wild, never to be allowed back among the Israelites. The scapegoat served to expiate the sins of Israel. By this act, their sins are removed.

Like the sacrificial goat, Christ is our sacrifice for sin. He died to pay its penalty. Like the scapegoat, Christ is the sin bearer. "He himself bore our sins in his body on the tree, so that we might die to sins and live for righteousness; by his wounds you have been healed" (1 Peter 2:24).

Describing Christ in Romans 3:25, Paul wrote: "God presented him as a sacrifice of atonement [literally, a propitiation], through faith in his blood." The Greek word that is translated "sacrifice of atonement" in this verse is *hilasterion*. In the Septuagint, the Greek translation of the Old Testament, the same word is used to describe the lid of the ark of the covenant. This lid is referred to as the "atonement cover" in some modern translations. Again the event of Leviticus 16 is in mind, with the sacrificial goat and the scapegoat—the former being propitiatory, the later being expiatory. It seems likely in Romans 3:25 Paul is linking these two activities into the single act of Christ. However, since the text grounds Christ's "propitiation" in faith in Christ's blood, it also seems reasonable to assume propitiation is the basis for expiation.

In short, Christ's death turns away God's wrath and removes our sin, thus paving the way for reconciliation. Theologian Leon Morris has made this case persuasively. He noted that God's wrath is mentioned 585 times in the Old Testament, so that words in the *hilaskomai* group simply cannot mean merely to "expiate" or cancel sin.[3] Since God's wrath is so inextricably tied to sin, any notion of atonement must involve satisfying God's wrath (cf. Rom. 1:18).

Redemption and Ransom

Christ's atonement is an act of redemption and ransom. Like expiation and propitiation, redemption and ransom are often linked, the former dealing with deliverance from bondage, the latter with payment in relation to the deliverance.

In the Old Testament, redemption is a powerful theme in the story of God's deliverance of Israel from Egypt in the days of Moses. In Exodus 6:2–8 God promised Moses that He would redeem Israel. The theme of redemption, especially Israel's redemption from slavery in Egypt, is repeated several places in the Old Testament. (See, for example, Ex. 15:13; Deut. 7:8; and Ps. 78:35.) What is interesting about the accounts of Israel's redemption in Exodus 6 and 15 is that it is redemption without ransom. God is not portrayed as "paying" Egypt in order to secure Israel's release. Israel's song of worship after the destruction of the Egyptian army at the Red Sea makes this clear. "Who among the gods is like you, O LORD? Who is like you—majestic in holiness, awesome in glory, working wonders? You stretched out your right hand and the earth swallowed them. In your unfailing love you will lead the people you have redeemed. In your strength you will guide them to your holy dwelling" (Ex. 15:11–13). God's redemption was grounded in His majesty and power, not payment.[4]

Other passages in the Old Testament link redemption and payment. This is seen especially in passages like Leviticus 25:47–49: "If an alien or a temporary resident among you becomes rich and one of your countrymen becomes poor and sells himself to the alien living among you or to a member of the alien's clan, he retains the right of redemption after he has sold himself. One of his relatives may redeem him: An uncle or a cousin or any blood relative in his clan may redeem him. Or if he prospers, he may redeem himself." In this case redemption was tied to the paying of a ransom.[5]

In the New Testament, four different Greek words lie behind the terms *redemption* and *ransom*. The basic idea is the concept of liberation, particularly as the result of a payment. One of the most widely used Greek words is *apolytrosis*. The word is used ten times in the New Testament. It carries the ideas of release, pardon, dismissal, and deliverance. It usually involves the paying of a ransom and has its roots in the Greek marketplace—particularly the slave trade.[6] However, in every case in the new Testament, a specific price or payment is neither mentioned nor necessary for understanding the text. It seems likely then that the authors of the New Testament were grounding their conception in the Old Testament events like the Exodus, rather than the cultural context of the slave market. As one theologian has put it, "While the idea of price is present in the New Testament, . . . it is more related to propitiation and sacrifice than to redemption or ransom."[7]

Charles Ryrie's summary on the subject of redemption probably states it best. "First, people are redeemed *from something* (the marketplace of sin). Second, they are redeemed *by something* (the blood of Christ). Third, they are redeemed *to something* (the freedom of slavery to the Lord). Redemption is viewed man ward; mankind was in slavery to sin and in need of release from bondage and slavery to sin."[8]

OBJECTIVE THEORIES OF ATONEMENT

Throughout its history, the church has proposed various theories to explain how Christ's death accomplished reconciliation. These were attempts to explain how Christ's death brought about reconciliation between God and humanity. Generally these theories have fallen into two categories. Some are "objective theories" because they assume there is some object between God and humanity. Thus the Atonement involves removing this object. Others are categorized as "subjective theories." These theories deny that there is some object that needs to be removed and argue that the purpose of the Atonement is to show us something about God. We will briefly look at three objective theories and three subjective theories.[9]

The Ransom Theory

One of the earliest theories proposed is the ransom theory, sometimes referred to as the "Christus Victor" or "classical" theory.[10] In essence, this theory argues that when Adam and Eve sinned, they sold themselves and their offspring into slavery to Satan. Therefore, a ransom had to be paid to Satan in order to free us. This ransom consisted of the death of Christ. Sometimes the "triumph" theme is tied to this theory. In those cases, Christ not only ransoms us, he triumphs over the powers of sin and death as well. This is an objective theory.

Ireneaus (A.D. 145–202) was one of the first to argue for this theory in his work *"Against Heresies."* According to Ireneaus, in order to be just, God had to pay Satan. Therefore, to simply overpower Satan and take humanity back would be unjust. Christ's death should thus be seen as a ransom paid to Satan.

Origen, a theologian from the third century, made a similar argument. He relied heavily on two texts from the New Testament, Matthew 20:28 and Mark 10:45, where Jesus is described as giving His life a ransom for many. Origen maintained that since Christ's death was a ransom, it raised an obvious question. To whom was this ransom paid? Since it made no sense as a payment to God, Origen reasoned it must have been a payment to Satan.[11]

Gregory of Nyssa, the great Cappadocian Father of the fourth century, further developed this argument. As humanity had sold themselves to Satan, God was obligated to respect Satan's right to us. Therefore, in order to get us back, God had to somehow get Satan to forfeit his rights to humanity. God accomplished this by luring Satan. Gregory used fishing imagery to make his point; in fact, he saw Job 41:1 ("Can you draw out Leviathan with a fishhook?") as foreshadowing the Atonement. He argued that God baited a hook for Satan, with Jesus' humanity serving as the worm and his deity as the hook. Satan was lured by the humanity of Christ and sought to assert his control over Him. Too late Satan found out that Jesus was not just human, but He was also divine. Therefore, Satan had overstepped his bounds and was forced to renounce his claim on humanity.[12]

While this theory is certainly colorful and quite dramatic, it is hard to defend biblically or morally. As we have seen, the language of redemption in the New Testament redemption is best understood as the language of propitiation rather than ransom. Further, the New Testament does not present Christ's death as primarily payment to Satan. Morally, the ransom to Satan theory tends to portray God as duping Satan to redeem us. This amounts to a sort of redemption by deception, hardly the sort of behavior one would expect from the God of the Bible.

Vicarious Satisfaction Theory

In the late eleventh century, Anselm, the archbishop of Canterbury, wrote what many consider the seminal work on the atonement. Entitled *Cur Deus Homo* ("Why God Became a Man"), Anselm's work marked a shift in thinking about the atonement and outlined what is known as the "vicarious satisfaction" theory. *Vicarious* means "in the place of" and *satisfaction* has to do with responding to dishonor brought about by an offense. Anselm saw the problem as being a function of God's honor and righteousness. He posed the question, How can the dishonor brought to God by sin be satisfied? For Anselm the problem did not revolve around how justice could be maintained in relation to Satan, but how God could be just to Himself and still save humanity.

Combining themes from the Incarnation with the Atonement, Anselm developed a detailed and thorough argument proving that a "God-Man" was necessary to accomplish human salvation. Alister McGrath has summarized it in the following way:

1. God created humanity in a state of original righteousness, with the objective of bringing humanity to a state of eternal blessedness.

2. That state of eternal blessedness is contingent upon human obedience to God. However, through sin, humanity is unable to achieve this necessary obedience, which appears to frustrate God's purpose in creating humanity in the first place.

3. In that it is impossible for God's purposes to be frustrated, there must be some means by which the situation can be remedied. However, the situation can only be remedied if a *satisfaction* is made for sin. In other words, something has to be done, by which the offense caused by human sin can be purged.

4. There is no way in which humanity can provide this necessary satisfaction. It lacks the resources which are needed. On the other hand, God possesses the resources needed to provide the required satisfaction.

5. A "God-man" would possess both the *ability* (as God) and the *obligation* (as a human being) to pay the required satisfaction. Therefore the incarnation takes place, in order that the required satisfaction may be made, and humanity redeemed.[13]

McGrath has noted the theory's flaws. He points out that Anselm believed that the debt one incurs is proportional to the being one has offended. Many scholars have argued that this is an idea that fits better with the feudal system of Anselm's day than the Bible. Also, Anselm's notion of satisfaction seemed to be grounded more in the medieval Catholic church's system of penance than Scripture. Nevertheless, Anselm represents a vital turn in the history of the doctrine of atonement. As McGrath puts it, "Anselm's insistence that God is totally and utterly obliged to act according to the principles of justice throughout the redemption of humanity marks a decisive break with the morality of the *Christus Victor* view. In taking up Anselm's approach, later writers were able to place it on a more secure foundation by grounding it in the general principles of law."[14]

Penal Substitution Theory

One of those later writers, a sixteenth-century German monk named Martin Luther, would shake the foundations of not only the medieval church but also all of medieval Europe. Driven by an intense sense of his own sin, Luther found peace by placing his hope in the finished work of Christ. Thus the doctrine that came to be referred to as "justification by faith alone" became a rallying cry for those who would eventually be known as "Protestants."[15] By the mid 1500s Luther was joined by others, most notably John Calvin. They argued that by faith (itself a gift from God) a man or woman is made to be "in Christ." In turn, by virtue of being "in Christ," Christ's righteousness is imputed or transferred to the sinner. Christ took on their penalty so that the person may take on His righteousness. This transaction transforms the individual from being an object of God's wrath, to an object of God's love (Rom. 1:18; 8:31–39). Or as Calvin put it, "Not only was salvation given to us through Christ, but, by his grace the Father is now favorable to us."[16]

Luther and Calvin continued in the tradition of Anselm, arguing that God's righteousness must be satisfied. In his most famous work, *The Institutes of the Christian Religion*, Calvin wrote, "This readily shows that Christ's grace is too much weakened unless we grant to his sacrifice the power of expiating, appeasing, and making satisfaction."[17] Luther and Calvin also emphasized Christ's death as a substitution, the innocent paying the penalty for the guilty. As such, these Reformers are often credited with formulating what has become known as the "penal substitution" theory of the atonement.

The difference in their emphasis relative to Anselm's was subtle but significant. The issue for the Reformers was not so much God's honor as it was God's holiness and justice. God's holiness and justice demand sin be punished. It was this that stood between God and humanity. Jesus made reconciliation possible by not only solving the problem of paying the penalty for sin, He also made an ongoing relationship possible by imputing His righteousness to the sinner by faith. God, the Holy one who cannot look on sin, can thus be reconciled to His wayward sinful creatures.

SUBJECTIVE THEORIES OF ATONEMENT

Abelard's Theory

A younger contemporary of Anselm, Peter Abelard (A.D. 1079–1142), proposed a theory in sharp distinction to the "vicarious atonement" approach of Anselm. Abelard centered his approach in the love of God, resting it on two biblical rails. One was Luke 7:47 where Jesus says, "Her many sins have been forgiven—for she loved much." The other text was Romans 3:24, which says that we are "justified freely," that is, as a gift. From this Abelard concluded that loving causes one to merit favor from God. Furthermore, he reasoned that God is free to forgive freely—no payment is necessary. Consequently, while humans cannot ultimately earn their salvation, Abelard believed Christ's merit completed the merit that humans accrue through love. Therefore, Christ's death is designed to teach us about God's love. By virtue of this extraordinary display of God's love, humans are moved to love God and each other more.[18]

This is a subjective theory; Christ's work is directed to humans with the goal of influencing their moral behavior. In essence, we are reconciled to God by being moved by Christ's example, and then following His example.

Socinus's Modification

Just as Luther and Calvin modified Anselm's theory of the atonement, two other thinkers continued in the subjective tradition of Abelard. Faustus Socinus (1539–1604) stayed close to Abelard, while Hugo Grotius (1583–1645) represented a more significant modification. Faustus Socinus was a radical thinker who rejected orthodox understandings of both the Trinity and human sinfulness. Specifically, he rejected the deity of Christ and original sin. He argued that human beings were capable of keeping God's law without any supernatural help and proposed a theory similar to Abelard's. Like Abelard, he rejected any form of satisfaction. Socinus wrote: "If we could get rid of this [idea that God's] justice [requires Him to punish sinners], even if we had no other proof, that fiction of Christ's satisfaction would be thoroughly exposed, and would vanish."[19] He maintained that God was free to forgive sinners without Christ's death. In that sense, for Socinus, Christ's death was not necessary.

However, since Socinus concluded that Christ's death was not a necessary component of forgiveness, he had to propose another purpose for His death. This is where his rejection of original sin came into play. Since humans can keep God's moral code, he suggested, Christ's death functions as an example or role for the human race to follow. Socinus's theory is often referred to as the "example theory."

Grotius's Theory

Hugo Grotius rejected Socinus's theory but continued in the subjective tradition. Like Abelard, he believed that God is free to forgive sins as He sees fit. However, Grotius grounded his view of the atonement in law and government, rather than in love as Abelard had done. For Grotius, God's freedom to forgive was a function of His role as ruler of the universe. Christ's death was a means to get people to understand the seriousness of sin. It was intended to show that the government of the sovereign God could not be blithely ignored without profound consequences. The Crucifixion illustrated the penalty that awaits all sinners. Therefore, its purpose was to cause all humans to repent of their disobedience to God and to turn in submission and obedience to God.

THE MODERNIST/
FUNDAMENTALIST PERIOD

No particular objective or subjective theory of atonement held sway over the years. However, the "penal-substitutionary" theory was embraced by the Puritans, who brought this perspective with them to colonial America. Jonathan Edwards, arguably America's most brilliant theologian, continued in this tradition. However, by the 1800s the prominent evangelist Charles G. Finney was proposing a subjective approach—the governmental theory. Consequently, a number of views were being espoused by evangelical Christians in the mid- to late nineteenth century. Just as diverse opinions about the atonement abounded, different ideas about sin, the Bible, and the person of Jesus began to be more broadly circulated. As the nineteenth century closed, sharp disagreements among Protestants arose on a number of issues, including the atonement.

Indeed, as the Protestant church in America entered the twentieth century, it found dissension among its ranks. Influenced by certain ideals from the Enlightenment in Europe and biblical criticism, particularly as German scholars were practicing it, some Protestants began rethinking key elements of Christian doctrine in an effort to make it more palatable to the modern mind. Thus they became known as "modernists" or "liberals."

Modernists began to question the deity of Christ and the authority of Scripture. They also questioned the doctrines of original sin and total depravity. This led to a dramatic revision in thinking about the purpose of the work of Christ. Jesus was increasingly presented by modernists as the perfect human, who stands as the ultimate example of what we should strive to be. They believed that He is what the human race is evolving toward. Drawing somewhat from Abelard and deeply from Socinus, modernists proposed a theory of atonement that was very subjective and grounded in a denial of original sin and the deity of Christ.

Conservative Christians responded with a reassertion of the historic Protestant position. Writing in *The Fundamentals,* Prof. Franklin Johnson and Rev. Dyson Hague reasserted the doctrine of substitutionary atonement. They argued along three basic lines. First, some form of satisfaction or substitutionary atonement has always been the historic position of the church. Second, only those views that center on substitutionary atonement are consistent with the majority of the biblical data on this subject. Third, much of the modernist approach is grounded in the heretical assertions of Socinus.[20]

IMPORTANCE OF THE ATONEMENT

How should we think about Christ's work as we begin the twenty-first century? What difference does it make? Any theory of the Atonement that minimizes the Bible's teaching on human sinfulness is unacceptable. Any attempt to understand the Atonement that eliminates concepts like *propitiation* or *sacrifice* is unbiblical. Therefore, any theological system that eliminates substitution or satisfaction from its theory of atonement is unacceptable.

Consequently, the conclusions one draws about the Atonement depend upon one's theology of sin. Why is punishment necessary, if we are not doing anything wrong? Or, while we may admit to "sin" in our lives, is not what constitutes sin a function of our own personal moral codes, not a universal divine law? What does Jesus' death mean, if I can improve myself through self-help techniques? Or what does Jesus' death mean if I determine what "sins" needed to be atoned for?

Writing a few years ago, George Barna, a researcher into Christian and secular attitudes, described the popular attitude toward sin this way: "While people accept the existence of 'sin,' they do not take it as seriously as they once did, nor do they accept rigid definitions of sinful behavior. . . . As Americans have become more self-focused and self-reliant, even in spiritual matters, they are willing to take credit for both the good and the bad in their lives—success as well as sin."[21]

Ironically, while Americans are struggling with seeing themselves as sinners, they do not seem to have much difficulty in viewing Jesus as a sinner! In a July 1995 survey, researcher Barna found that 44 percent of respondents said that they believed that Jesus was human and committed sins like other people. Even more troubling, slightly more than a quarter (26 percent) of those who said that they had embraced Christ as their Savior also said they believed that He committed sins during His time on earth.[22] The implications of such a view for the Atonement are dramatic —they speak of a sinful Christ atoning for a not so sinful humanity. This is hardly the biblical picture and reveals the need for a renewed emphasis upon this important doctrine. Otherwise, we will soon find that we have reduced Christ's work of atonement to a mere example.

In many respects, we find ourselves at the beginning of this century in a similar situation as our forefathers a century ago. As the biblical teaching concerning human sinfulness becomes increasingly unpopular, will we be willing to hold our ground? Or will we, like the modernists, try to court popularity by changing our theology of the Atonement?

A related issue is the exclusiveness of Christ. Historically, the church has proclaimed that Jesus is not merely a Savior but that He is the only Savior. This claim is intimately related to Christ's work of atonement. As we have seen, truly nothing but the blood of Jesus can wash away human sin. Anselm argued that only a God-Man could atone for humanity. Luther and Calvin agreed. This sort of exclusive claim is increasingly under fire. There is evidence that many today do not see a link between spending eternity in heaven and the atoning work of Christ.[23] According to another Barna study, fully 46 percent believe that "all good people, whether or not they consider Jesus Christ to be their savior, will live in heaven after they die on earth."[24] The evangelical church must boldly proclaim the biblical doctrines of human sinfulness and a theology of substitutionary atonement that includes the ideas of sacrifice and propitiation and the full deity of Christ.

At the same time, a biblical balance must be maintained. It is possible to focus on substitutionary themes to the exclusion of others. Gordon Lewis and Bruce Demarest have compared the atonement to a "multifaceted" diamond:

> Illustrations of the atonement point up its different aspects. Analogies implied in biblical teaching refer to substitutionary sacrifice at an altar, acquittal in court, liberation from a slave market, victory on a battlefield, the embrace of reconciled enemies, the relationships of a new family, and inner peace. Thoughts about Christ's atonement are impoverished if they are limited to one of these models: sacrificial, judicial, experiential, or relational. Sin is not justly atoned for by a mere feeling of at-one-ment with the world or a mystical union with the cosmos. Sin is not sufficiently atoned for by a mere judicial decree of acquittal without personal reconciliation to God or experiential deliverance from bondage to unrighteousness. Neither is sin adequately atoned for by a mere liberation from

the slave market of sin (in a battlefield of temptation) without divine forgiveness and reconciliation. An integrative concept of the atonement seeks to incorporate the biblically supported facets that the historical views affirm while avoiding their exclusivistic negations.[25]

If the Fall was "multifaceted" in the sense that it affected all of our being and all of the created order, then its atonement must in turn be "multifaceted" as well.[26] This approach seeks to preserve the richness of the biblical data and its historical interpretations.

The atonement of Christ has implications in a number of issues, if we are willing to embrace the richness of the doctrine as it is presented in the Scriptures. Economics, racial relations, and ecological concerns are just a few areas that should be explored from the perspective of the Atonement. A biblical application of concepts of reconciliation may provide a new way to understand these issues. In that sense the church has hardly begun to plumb the depths of the doctrine of atonement.

The opposition we face may appear daunting, but it is certainly no more daunting than the opposition our forefathers faced a century ago. Like them, let us stand firm as we embrace the truth and "contend for the faith that was once for all entrusted to the saints" (Jude 3) by boldly proclaiming that nothing but the blood of Jesus can wash away human sin. Only Christ can reconcile fallen humanity and the Triune God.

NOTES

1. Robert Lowry, "What Can Wash Away My Sin?" verse 1. In public domain.
2. For some of the ideas in this section, I am indebted to Gerry Breshears, "Boundaries on Atonement Theology: Is There a Bottom Line?" a paper presented to the Evangelical Theology Society's annual meeting, November 14–16, 2001, Colorado Springs, Colorado.
3. Leon Morris, *The Apostolic Preaching of the Cross* (Grand Rapids: Eerdmans, 1956) and *The Cross in the New Testament* (Grand Rapids: Eerdmans, 1965); esp. Leon Morris, "The Use of Hilaskesthai in Biblical Greek," *Expository Times* (1950–1951): 233.

4. For some of the ideas in this section, I am indebted to Gerry Breshears, "Boundaries on Atonement Theology."
5. For other examples involving payment, see Ex. 13:12–16; 21:28–30; Num. 3:12–13; 8:16–17; 18:15–16.
6. Walter Bauer, Frederick William Danker, W. F. Arndt, and F. Wilbur Gingerich, *A Greek-English Lexicon of the New Testament* (Chicago: Univ. of Chicago, 1983), 95. For a detailed discussion of the meaning of various biblical terms, see Leon Morris, *The Apostolic Preaching of the Cross.*
7. Breshears, "Boundaries on Atonement Theology," n.p.
8. Charles C. Ryrie, *Basic Theology* (Wheaton, Ill.: Victor, 1986), 291–92.
9. I am indebted to Ted M. Dorman, *A Faith for All Seasons,* rev. ed. (Nashville: Broadman, 1995), for the idea for the structure of this section. See chapter 9.
10. For a good discussion of this theory, see Gustav Aulen, *Christus Victor* (New York: Macmillan, 1951). See also J. N. D. Kelly, *Early Christian Doctrines* (San Francisco: Harper & Row, 1960).
11. Alister E. McGrath, *Christian Theology,* 2d ed. (Malden, Mass.: Blackwell, 1997), 395. He writes the following; "Now it was the devil that held us, to whose side we had been drawn away by our sins. He asked, therefore, as our price the blood of Christ . . . so precious that alone it sufficed for the redemption of all."
12. Gregory of Nyssa, *Great Catechisms,* chap. 24; as cited in Aulen, *Christus Victor,* 52.
13. McGrath, *Christian Theology,* 400–401.
14. Ibid., 402.
15. This is not to say justification by faith alone was the only or even main doctrinal difference between those who became known as Protestants and Roman Catholics. Perhaps even more crucial was the debate about the authority of the Bible relative to the papacy and church councils. For a survey of some of these debates, see Alister E. McGrath, *Reformation Thought: An Introduction,* 3d ed. (Malden, Mass.: Blackwell, 1999).
16. John Calvin, *The Institutes of the Christian Religion* (2.17.5), ed. John T. McNeill, trans. Ford Lewis Battles (Philadelphia: Westminster, 1977), 533.
17. Ibid., 532.
18. For a more detailed discussion, see Aulen, *Christus Victor,* 95–98.
19. William G. T. Shedd, *History of Christian Doctrine,* vol. 2, 376 n. 1 (New York: Scribner, 1863); as cited in Dorman, *A Faith for All Seasons,* 206.
20. Franklin Johnson, "The Atonement," vol. 2, chap. 5, and Dyson Hague, "At-One-Ment by Propitiation," vol. 2, chap. 6; ed. R. A. Torrey and A. C. Dixon, *The Fundamentals: A Testimony to the Truth* (Chicago: n. d.).
21. George Barna, *The Index of Leading Spiritual Indicators* (Dallas: Word, 1996), 22.
22. Ibid., 20.
23 Ibid., 72. Barna comments, "Americans have managed, intellectually, to separate the concepts of the forgiveness of sins—which they believe is possible only through the cleansing work of Christ—and the reception of eternal salvation—which they do not believe to be dependent upon the atonement of Christ."
24. Ibid.
25. Gordon Lewis and Bruce Demarest, *Integrative Theology* (Grand Rapids: Zondervan, 1996), 401–8.
26. Ibid., 408.

Gregg Quiggle is professor of theology at the Moody Bible Institute, where he teaches in the fields of church history, historical theology, philosophy, and apologetics. He holds degrees from Wheaton College and Marquette University in Milwaukee, Wisconsin, and is completing studies for a Ph.D. degree at the Open University in Milton Keynes, Great Britain.

6

RISEN AND COMING KING

THE BODILY RESURRECTION AND PHYSICAL RETURN OF JESUS CHRIST

Kevin D. Zuber

The resurrection of Jesus Christ from the dead is *the* fundamental truth of the Christian faith. Hundreds of theologians and apologists of the Christian faith have made this bold assertion, from the apostle Paul up until the present day. Those who have taken up the matter have found it difficult to express, with sufficient vigor and conviction, the crucial import of the truth claim, "He is risen!" It has been called "the very citadel of the Christian position."

R. A. Torrey noted, "While the literal bodily resurrection of Jesus Christ is the corner-stone of Christian doctrine, it is also the Gibraltar of Christian evidence, and the Waterloo of infidelity and rationalism. If the Scriptural assertions of Christ's resurrection can be established as historic certainties, the claims and doctrines of Christianity rest upon an impregnable foundation."[1] Echoing Torrey, one commentator called Christ's resurrection "the Gibraltar [upon which] the Christian man has entrenched himself."[2] Others have called it the "crowning proof," the "foundation," and the "centerpiece" of Christianity.[3] One popular Christian author wrote, "The doctrine of the resurrection [of Christ] is central in the Christian faith, not peripheral. To deny it is to remove the keystone of the arch of Christianity."[4]

These are not just the opinions of writers and scholars. The vital importance of the Resurrection was reflected in the preaching of the apostles from the very beginning of the Christian church. This theme was so important to the church's life and message that when the apostles set out to replace Judas, they determined that his successor had to be someone whose long-standing association with Jesus would qualify him as "a witness with us of his resurrection" (Acts 1:22).[5] Preaching and testifying to the Resurrection was the key function of an apostle. The sermons recorded in Acts bear this out. The thesis and applications of Peter's sermon in Acts 2:22–36, the first sermon of the church age, were grounded upon the fact of the bodily resurrection. Peter's response to the Jewish religious leaders after they ordered him not to teach in Jesus' name emphasized his responsibility as a witness of the Resurrection (Acts 5:29–32). Peter's message at the house of Cornelius noted that the apostles had been chosen to testify of the risen Christ (Acts 10:39–41).

The apostle Paul, likewise, made the Resurrection the focal point of his preaching. In his message to the Jews in Pisidian Antioch, Paul affirmed of the once crucified Christ, "But God raised him from the dead" (Acts 13:30). This was in fulfillment of the promise made to the fathers (Acts 13:32–34). Paul also preached the Resurrection to the Epicurean and Stoic philosophers in Athens (Acts 17:18, 22–31). These references to the resurrection of Jesus Christ in the testimony and preaching of the apostles are strong indications of the doctrine's importance for the preaching of the gospel.

THE WATERSHED TEXT

One of the most important New Testament texts that deals with the resurrection of Christ is 1 Corinthians 15:12–20, where Paul addressed some of the false teaching in the church at Corinth. Some members of the church at Corinth may have been Jews influenced by the teaching of the Sadducees, a sect that denied the bodily resurrection.[6] Others have suggested some of the Corinthian believers were enamored of Greek philosophy, which "believed in the immortality of the soul but rejected the resurrection of the body."[7] There may even have been a hint of Gnostic teaching in Corinth.[8] Whatever the source, the substance of the error is clear. Some were denying the bodily resurrection of the dead (1 Cor. 15:12). Although they did not deny Christ's resurrection explicitly, they did deny a general resurrection of humanity and the bodily resurrection of believers at the end of the age.

Paul countered this error with devastating candor and impeccable logic, listing the inevitable implications of such teaching. The most important was the assertion found in 1 Corinthians 15:13: "If there is no resurrection of the dead, then not even Christ has been raised." The very form of this sentence insists upon its own denial.[9] In the subsequent verses, the apostle Paul spelled out the consequences that must inevitably follow if such a thing were to be true. First, if Christ did not rise from the dead, then the gospel that Paul had preached was "useless" (1 Cor. 15:14). The "good news" was in effect "no news" or "empty news." Second, if Christ did not rise, then the faith of the Corinthians was also "vain." In short, it meant that they have believed in "nothing." Third, if Christ did not rise from the dead, it meant that those who claimed that He had were liars: "More than that, we are then found to be false witnesses about God, for we have testified about God that he raised Christ from the dead. But he did not raise him if in fact the dead are not raised" (1 Cor. 15:15).

Verse 15 actually contains two consequences in one. If Christ did not rise, then anyone who testifies that Christ has been raised from the dead is a liar. Moreover, those who claim that He did rise attribute to God something that God did not do.

The fourth consequence of the Corinthian claim that there was no such thing as bodily resurrection was equally serious. If Christ did not rise from the dead, then all who had placed their faith in Him were still in their sins (1 Cor. 15:17). Glancing back over the previous context, where he had noted that the burial and the death of Christ was "for our sins," the apostle concluded that to deny one was to deny all (1 Cor. 15:3–4). In such a case, the "faith" exercised is pointless and yields no justification and no sanctification. As Gordon Fee explained,

> The denial of their future, that they have been destined for resurrection on the basis of Christ's resurrection, has the net effect of a denial of their past, that they received forgiveness of sins on the basis of Christ's death. As in Rom. 4:25 and 5:10, the death of Jesus as "for us," including justification and sanctification, is inextricably bound together with his resurrection.[10]

Their denial of the Resurrection was a costly one, contrary to their experience as those "who have been sanctified in Christ Jesus, saints by calling" (1 Cor. 1:2 NASB). However, not yet finished with his argument, Paul added a fifth, devastating consequence. If Christ was not raised, "then those also who have fallen asleep in Christ are lost" (1 Cor. 15:18). The euphemism of "sleep" when applied to saints is one that is quite clear in Paul's writings. Those "asleep" are those who have died (cf. 1 Thess. 4:13–16). If there is no resurrection, then all those who had died were still in their sins. They had not entered into God's presence but were forever cut off from Him as the just penalty for their sins. They were gone, separated from all contact with loved ones left behind, forever. It is no wonder that Paul concluded with the assertion of verse 19: "If only for this life we have hope in Christ, we are to be pitied more than all men."

As Gordon Fee has noted, "There seems to be little hope of getting around Paul's argument, that to deny Christ's resurrection is tantamount to a denial of Christian existence altogether."[11]

JESUS' TEACHING ON THE RESURRECTION

By emphasizing the importance of the Resurrection to the gospel message, Paul did no more than Jesus did Himself. Jesus made the Resurrection a truth of crucial significance. For example, when asked to justify His action of driving the money changers from the temple, Jesus offered this "sign": "Destroy this temple, and I will raise it again in three days" (John 2:19b). In the next verses John clarified that Jesus was not talking about the literal temple but was speaking of the temple of His body (John 2:20–21). Jesus tied the fact of the Resurrection to His own defense of His authority and person. In effect He was saying, "You will know My authority and the veracity of My claims when I am raised from the dead."

He made the same point when the scribes and Pharisees asked Him for a sign in Matthew 12:38–41. Jesus replied that the only sign they would receive was "the sign of the prophet Jonah." He explained that as Jonah was three days and three nights in the belly of the fish, "so the Son of Man will be three days and three nights in the heart of the earth" (Matt. 12:40). Jesus tied His messianic claim to the Resurrection and taught that "the mighty event of [his] glorious resurrection should cause all men to repent."[12]

There are other indications of the importance Jesus placed upon the Resurrection. After the Transfiguration, He instructed

His disciples to tell no one about the vision "until the Son of Man has been raised from the dead" (Matt. 17:9; cf. Mark 9:9). While there may have been several reasons for the disciples to keep this "messianic secret," one surely was that it was only after the Resurrection that the significance of the Transfiguration could be properly understood. In this and other instances in which Jesus foretold His death and resurrection, there was a clear expectation on the part of Jesus of His resurrection. By making these statements, Jesus effectively staked His credibility on this event. It can hardly be claimed, therefore, that the Resurrection was only of incidental significance to Jesus. In person, in action, and by way of instruction, He is the fountainhead of the claim that the resurrection of Jesus Christ is *the* fundamental truth of the Christian faith.

CAN WE PROVE THE RESURRECTION?

Most challenges to the bodily resurrection of Christ dissolve when one accepts the inspiration and authority of the Bible. In nearly every case, intellectual and philosophical presuppositions underlie the theories and reconstructions of the historical Jesus. Enlightenment rationalism gave way to existentialism, which in turn has given way to postmodern relativism. Critical scholars were not (and are not) unbiased inquirers and seekers after the truth.[13]

In view of this, how can we who hold to the inspiration and truth of the Bible prove the Resurrection in the light of critical scholarship, whose basic presupposition is that the Gospel records are historically unreliable? Or indeed, how can we talk about proof to the average person, whose knowledge of Jesus is often drawn more from television specials and popular magazines than from the Bible? How can we "prove" the Resurrection to someone with naturalistic, anti-supernaturalistic, or postmodern presuppositions?

Recognizing Contrasting Worldviews

The short answer, in all candor, is that we cannot. At least, not as long as those who reject the truth of the Resurrection refuse to acknowledge the degree to which their worldview controls the outcome of the discussion. If someone begins with the "knowledge" that the dead do not, under any conditions, come back to life, or that no truth claim can make others false, then no amount of "proof" from history or even evidence from the Bible (construed as merely historical evidence) will convince the person otherwise. Too often during debates between conservative and liberal scholars about the Resurrection, both parties simply talk past one another. One respondent to just such a debate has written, "What shapes the debate . . . more than anything else, it seems to me, is the . . . 'conceptual incommensurability of [the] rival arguments.' What is at issue [are] . . . the claims of conflicting worldviews."[14] When those engaged in debate fail to acknowledge one another's worldview, they simply repeat their arguments, as if the other side has not heard them.

If this is true, however, it is true on both sides of the discussion. Evangelicals, like those who oppose them, also argue from presuppositions that shape the outcome of the debate.[15] This would not be a problem, if it were not for the fact that we often present our case as if we were operating from some neutral, value-free zone, objectively examining the evidence. Alan G. Padgett writes that this approach is "a powerful and influential myth, arising from the Enlightenment divorce of religion and science, which assumes that a purely neutral, value-free 'scientific' approach to the historical Jesus is desirable and possible." Padgett advises scholars to "take off the mask of pure objectivity" and "embrace our faith and recognize it for what it is."[16] It would be more honest if we were to acknowledge our faith commitment up front. Furthermore, since we are using the Word of God as evidence, we might be more effective if we acknowledge from the very start that it *is* God's Word (Heb. 4:12; Isa. 55:11)!

Considering the Resurrection and the Cross

In addition, we must be recognize that the historical fact of the Resurrection cannot be separated from the theological fact of the Resurrection. If it is to mean anything at all, the event of the Resurrection cannot be separated from the event of the Cross. It was the crucified Jesus Christ who is the eternal Son of the living God who was raised. As theologian Wolfhart Pannenberg has observed, "We cannot detach the fact of the resurrection from its meaning."[17] Even if one could succeed in convincing others of the bare historical fact, it would have no meaning without the theological fact.[18] Thomas F. Torrance makes the point:

> In other words, we can interpret the resurrection only if we interpret it theologically as well as historically. It will not do, however, to interpret it merely "theologically" as if it could be done apart from history, for that would mythologize and docetize it, and then we would have nothing to interpret. Nor can we interpret it merely "historically" in the sense that we interpret other historical events in human history, only by reference to human agency and natural processes, for that would be tantamount to insisting that all we have here is an ordinary historical happening, and [thus tantamount] to rejecting from the start the claim that the Agent is the Son of God. . . . It is incumbent upon us to interpret the resurrection as [an] historical event in accordance with the nature of the Agent or Subject concerned.[19]

Does it make any sense, then, to talk about "proving the Resurrection"? Such debates do, at least, have the potential to help others recognize how their worldview has predetermined the outcome of the discussion. Moreover, they show that if one begins with the Christian worldview, the presentation of the evidence is more than compelling. It is possible to talk about proof of the bodily resurrection of Christ, so long as the data is presented from a conscientiously Christian theistic worldview that accepts the Bible as the inspired and inerrant Word of God. Within that worldview the evidence of the empty tomb, the appearances of Jesus to His disciples, and the transformation of the disciples are both convincing and compelling.

Such evidences may not be "proof" for the scholar or for the average person whose view of Jesus has been shaped by the popularization of skeptical scholarship such as the Jesus Seminar. But by presenting the evidence from a Christian theistic worldview, one does at least have the opportunity to expose their (probably) unacknowledged worldview and to reveal their prejudices and biases regarding this subject. It also provides us with an opportunity to demonstrate the superior explanatory power of the Christian worldview when it comes to the question of the bodily resurrection of Jesus Christ.

THE REALITY OF CHRIST'S RESURRECTION

There would be no need for the Resurrection if Christ did not actually die. The Gospels and the rest of the New Testament are quite clear on this point. For instance, Matthew 27:50 records: "And when Jesus had cried out again in a loud voice, he gave up his spirit." This is clearly meant to convey the fact that Jesus died.[20] In his account, Matthew moves naturally from recording Jesus' speaking from the cross, to mentioning women who were ministering "to him," and to referring to the body of Jesus (Matt. 27:59–60). The action of placing the body in a tomb presumes that Jesus was dead. The request of the priests that Pilate make Jesus' tomb secure assumed that Jesus had died and was prompted by the fear that His disciples might steal the corpse

(Matt. 27:62–66). There is nothing in the account to indicate any other conclusion than that Jesus was dead.

The other Gospel accounts bear this same straightforward and uncontrived style of recording the event of Jesus' death (Mark 15:42–47; Luke 23:44–56; John 19:23–42). Of particular note is John's account, which includes several significant details that make the point even more solidly. For example, John notes that a spear was thrust into Jesus' side. This action was precipitated by the discovery by the soldiers that "he was already dead" (John 19:33). The Roman soldiers of the first century were men well acquainted with death by warfare and by execution. It is unlikely that they would have been mistaken in this case. Second, they thrust the spear into Jesus' side to ensure that His death was certain even if they had been in error. There can be little question as to the significance of the notation. As Carson puts it, "However the medical experts work this out, there can be little doubt that the Evangelist is emphasizing Jesus' death, his death as a man, his death beyond a shadow of a doubt."[21]

In addition, it should be noted that all these accounts indicate incontrovertibly that it was *Jesus* who died. The man who died on the cross was the same Jesus who was the leader of the disciples and the enemy of the Jewish authorities. Luke 23:35 indicates that He was recognized by the authorities and Luke 23:49 identifies His followers as being "from Galilee." John even indicates some of His relatives were present at the Crucifixion (John 19:25–26). The inescapable conclusion is that it was Jesus of Nazareth who died. This is obviously an important piece of information in and of itself but it is so additionally because it deals decisively with some of the views that have been posited with respect to the Resurrection. For instance, it demolishes the "swoon theory." Against those who suggest that His death was wrongly assumed, or even purposely faked or that He only "seemed" to be dead, comes the simple testimony of the Gospel writer that when Jesus' side was pierced it produced "a sudden flow of blood and water" (John 19:34).[22] The plain and unapologetic sense of the Gospel records is that He was not just weak, unconscious, and "apparently dead," as the Docetists argued and as Islam still argues, but that he was truly dead.[23]

Furthermore, this fact dismisses any idea that a substitute or twin took His place on the cross.[24] As noted, John records that Jesus' mother, aunt, and even the beloved disciple himself were all present at the Crucifixion (John 19:25–27). It is inconceivable that they would mistake Jesus for even a close "look-alike." And it is implausible that the scene depicted was part of a charade to cover up a deception. There is no evidence of such a conspiracy anywhere in the accounts (or anywhere else for that matter). The account itself is simple and candid and gives no indication of being anything other than what it is: a moving episode between a distraught mother watching her son be cruelly killed while He selflessly takes thought for her continuing care. In short, it simply does not read like a cover story for a fraud. Alternative explanations lack credibility while the Gospel accounts are eminently credible. Any denial of Jesus' death is therefore to be rejected.

THE NATURE OF CHRIST'S RESURRECTION

A Unique Event

At this point it is necessary to consider the nature of the Resurrection as it is described in the Gospels. Three key features must be understood. First, this was a unique event. It was a resurrection, not a resuscitation as in the case of Lazarus. As E. P. Sanders noted, the people of the first century were familiar with "two phenomena that are similar to resurrection: ghosts and resuscitated corpses." Sanders notes, "Both Luke and Paul opposed the idea that the risen Lord was a ghost."[25] Luke explicitly says this in Luke 24:37–40 (citing the words of Jesus), and Paul makes the same point by implication in his statements in 1 Corinthians 15. Furthermore, Sanders observed that they were equally opposed to the idea that Jesus was a resuscitated corpse. While stories of such resuscitations were current in their day, "Paul and Luke, however, denied that the risen Lord was simply resuscitated."[26]

Luke takes some effort to describe the physical body of the risen Christ as the same yet different. In Luke 24:37 (NASB) he notes that the disciples at first "[thought] they were seeing a spirit." This would indicate that this is not just a revivified body. He quotes Jesus saying, "Why are you troubled, and why do doubts rise in your minds? Look at my hands and my feet. It is I myself! Touch me and see; a ghost does not have flesh and bones, as you see I have" (vv. 38–39). Clearly, some of their astonishment was due to the fact that Jesus had died but now stood before them alive.

It may be noted that nowhere in this text (or in the other accounts) are there any details that might indicate that this was just a revived Jesus. His wounds, while visible, do not appear to have limited His movement, and He gives no other indications that He is in "recovery." This was not a rejuvenated body but something much more refined. Furthermore, Paul refers to Christ as "the firstfruits" (1 Cor. 15:20, 23). It is evident from the context that the apostle's point is primarily that because Christ has been raised, "the resurrection of the believing dead is absolutely inevitable; it has been guaranteed by God himself."[27] But it is also true that Paul could not have made this assurance, in just these terms, if Jesus' resurrection was not the very first of its kind.[28] The Scriptures record others who were restored to life prior to this, yet each one died again, including the sons of the widow of Zarephath and the Shunamite (1 Kings 17:17–24; 2 Kings 4:17–27), the daughter of Jairus (Mark 5:22–43), the young man of Nain (Luke 7:11–17), and Lazarus (John 11). Jesus' resurrection was unique because He is "alive forevermore" (Rev. 1:18 NASB).

A Supernatural Event

The resurrection of Christ was also supernatural. The Bible leaves no question in this regard when it asserts that God raised Him from the dead (Acts 3:15; cf. 2:24; Rom. 8:11; Eph. 1:20; Col. 2:12; cf. 1 Peter 3:18). To say the Resurrection was supernatural is just to say that the mechanism that accomplished it and the explanation of the event itself is "beyond the realm of sense experience" and "transcends the powers of nature."[29] In short, natural processes cannot explain or reproduce the Resurrection.

A Resurrected Body

Third, the resurrection of Jesus was physical and bodily. In many ways this is the crux of the matter and the point at issue with respect to the meaning of the empty tomb and the significance of the Resurrection appearances. The evidence of the New Testament accounts of the resurrection of Christ make it clear that it was physical and bodily in nature.[30] After His resurrection Jesus was touched by human hands and extended the invitation to others to touch Him (Matt. 28:9; Luke 24:39; John 20:17, 27). A spirit, ghost, or vision cannot be touched. Jesus affirmed that He had flesh and bones (Luke 24:39). What is more, Jesus ate food on at least four occasions (Luke 24:30, 41–43; John 21:12–13; Acts 1:4). In Luke 24:41 we are told that He made a special point to eat some fish in order to prove that He was with them bodily.

Further proof of the bodily nature of the Resurrection comes in Jesus' comments about His scars, clearly visible after the Crucifixion (John 20:20, 25–29; see Ps. 22:16). Jesus Himself pointed to the wounds to convince and comfort the disciples and to rebuke Thomas for not believing the testimony of the others. He obviously thought this was strong proof that He Himself, and He bodily, had been raised from the dead. Other Scripture references indicate that these same scars will identify Christ at His Second Coming (Rev. 1:7; 5:6; Zech. 12:10).

Jesus' body was recognized by those who had known Him before the Crucifixion (Matt. 28:7, 17; Mark 16:7; John 20:16; 1 Cor. 9:1). It could be seen and heard (Matt. 28:17; Luke 24:31–32).

WHAT DOES THE RESURRECTION PROVE?

Evidence for the Gospel's Truth

When one examines in the book of Acts sermons of the early church, every reference to the resurrection of Christ is given as evidence for the truth of the gospel; never is the Resurrection cited as something that must be proven. Peter's sermon in Acts 2, for instance, had as its thesis that Jesus of Nazareth who was crucified is "both Lord and Christ" (Acts 2:36). The proof of this was the Resurrection (Acts 2:31). The same point was made in Peter's sermon in Acts 4:8–12 and Paul's sermon in Acts 13:16–41. Even in the foreshortened message in Acts 17, Paul intended to drive home his thesis by reference to the proof given to all, namely, that God had raised Jesus from the dead (Acts 17:31).

In a sense, the Resurrection is proof of the Christian faith itself. Since Jesus Christ has been raised bodily from the dead, it follows that:

- There is a resurrection of believers to come (1 Cor. 15:12; cf. 1 Thess. 4:13–18).
- There is a life-changing dynamic to the preaching of the gospel (Rom 10:9–11; 1 Cor. 15:13; 2 Cor. 5:17).
- We have forgiveness of sin, are justified, and have been reconciled to God (Rom 3:21–28; 5:1–10; 1 Cor. 15:17).
- We know that to be absent from the body is *not* to perish but to be present with the Lord (2 Cor. 5:1–9).

- We know that life, joy, peace, purpose, and eternal life are ours and that those outside of Christ are the ones who ought to be pitied (1 Cor. 15:19; John 14:1–3; cf. 1 Cor. 15:51–58).

Evidence for the Truth of Jesus' Words

The Resurrection is important because it verifies all that Jesus claimed to be true about Himself (cf. John 2:13–22; Matt. 12:38–40). As theologian B. B. Warfield wrote, "Our Lord himself deliberately staked his whole claim upon the resurrection."[31] The bodily resurrection of Christ is a fundamental of the Christian faith because all of Christ's claims, teachings, and promises rest upon it. "Had Christ not risen," Warfield observed, "we could not believe him to be what he declared himself when he 'made himself equal with God.'"[32] With the Resurrection, we can have a vital faith and accept the integrity of the gospel message.

The Resurrection offers a vital confirmation of Christ's work. Paul made this clear when he declared that Jesus "was delivered over to death for our sins and was raised to life for our justification" (Rom. 4:25). The Resurrection is the evidence that God has accepted the sacrificial work of Christ. The Resurrection also is the proof that Jesus is

- the Messiah (Acts 2:32–36),
- the "Son of Man" (Matt. 17:22–23),
- the "Lord and Christ" (Acts 2:22–36; cf. Eph. 1:20–21),
- the coming judge of all (Acts 10:39–42), and
- most vital, the Son of God; Paul says explicitly that Jesus "was declared with power to be the Son of God by his resurrection from the dead" (Rom. 1:4).

Evidence That Jesus Will Return

Finally, the bodily resurrection of Jesus Christ guarantees that He will come again. The Bible clearly teaches that Jesus Christ will return. He Himself promised to return (Matt. 24:30; John 14:1–3). The angels present at the Ascension foretold His return (Acts 1:10–11). The apostles taught and anticipated His return (Acts 3:19–21; 1 Thess. 4:13–18; 1 Tim. 6:14–15). Entire books of the New Testament were written around the theme of His return (2 Thessalonians; Revelation). We are taught to pray for His return (Rev. 22:20). But it is the bodily resurrection that makes it possible for Christ's return to be truly physical.

The Scriptures teach that Jesus will return physically to receive the church (John 14:1–6; 1 Thess. 4:13–18). Paul's description of Christ's return in 1 Thessalonians 4 indicates that this will be both a personal and a physical event. The apostle John noted that at that time "we shall see him as he is" (1 John 3:2). Jesus will return physically to judge the living and the dead (Acts 10:42). This judgment will take place in the physical presence of Jesus Christ, "at his appearing" (2 Tim. 4:1). J. Dwight Pentecost explained:

> Repeated references in the Scriptures establish the fact that the second advent will be a full and visible manifestation of the Son of God to the earth (Acts 1:11; Rev. 1:7; Matt. 24:30). As the son was publicly repudiated and rejected, He shall be publicly presented by God at the second advent. This advent will be associated with the visible manifestation of glory (Matt. 16:27; 25:31), for in the completion of judgment and the manifestation of sovereignty God is glorified (Rev. 14:7; 18:1; 19:1).[33]

Jesus will return physically in order to establish His kingdom in fulfillment of the many Old Testament covenantal promises to Israel. He will return to occupy the throne of David (Ps. 2:6). This will be in fulfillment of the promise made to David in 2 Samuel 7:4–17. This promise must be fulfilled literally and such a fulfillment requires the physical return of Christ.[34] The kingdom that Christ will establish is described in many Old Testament contexts as a literal earthly kingdom with definite "economic, social and physical aspects."[35] In order to reign over such a kingdom, Christ must have a literal physical existence. The hope of Christ's return and future reign are not merely guaranteed by His resurrection, they demand it.

It is not saying too much, then, to assert that the bodily resurrection of Jesus Christ is *the* fundamental truth of the Christian faith. Everything that we experience and hope for in the Christian life depends upon it. With the Resurrection comes the gospel, the church, and our ultimate hope. In view of this, it is no wonder that Christians down through the ages have worshiped their Savior and celebrated their faith with this triumphant cry: "He is risen! He is risen indeed!"

NOTES

1. R. A. Torrey, "The Certainty and Importance of the Bodily Resurrection of Jesus Christ from the Dead," in *The Fundamentals* (reprint, Grand Rapids: Baker, 2000), 2:299.
2. Benjamin B. Warfield, "The Resurrection of Christ: A Fundamental Doctrine," ed. John E. Meeter, *Selected Shorter Writings of Benjamin B. Warfield* (Grand Rapids: Baker, 1970), 1:193.
3. Henry M. Morris, *Many Infallible Proofs* (San Diego: Creation Life Publishers, 1974), 88–89; Simon J. Kistemaker, *I Corinthians* (Grand Rapids: Baker, 1993), 525.
4. J. Oswald Sanders, *The Incomparable Christ* (Chicago: Moody, 1971), 223.
5. Richard N. Longenecker, "The Acts of the Apostles," *The Expositor's Bible Commentary*, ed. Frank E. Gaebelein (Grand Rapids: Zondervan, 1981), 9:265.
6. See Mark 12:18; also Donald A. Hagner, "Sadducees," in ed. Merrill C. Tenney, *The Zondervan Pictorial Encyclopedia of the Bible* (Grand Rapids: Zondervan, 1975), 5:214–15.
7. Gordon D. Fee, *The First Epistle to the Corinthians* (Grand Rapids: Eerdmans, 1987), 715–16; see also Diogenes Allen, *Philosophy for Understanding Theology* (Atlanta: John Knox, 1985), 56–59; Kistemaker, *I Corinthians*, 540; and John F. MacArthur, *1 Corinthians* (Chicago: Moody, 1984), 408.

8. See Andrew F. Walls, "Gnosticism," *The Zondervan Pictorial Encyclopedia of the Bible,* vol. 2 (Grand Rapids: Zondervan, 1975), 738.

9. Kistemaker, *I Corinthians,* 541; "With the double negative in the two parts of this verse, Paul writes a conditional sentence that is contrary to reality."

10. Fee, *The First Epistle to the Corinthians,* 743–44.

11. Ibid., 745. Fee adds, "Yet many do so—to make the faith more palatable to 'modern man,' we are told. But that will scarcely do. What modern man accepts in its place is no longer the Christian faith." The rest of this paragraph ought to be read as well. Suffice it to say that I think Fee puts his finger on the motive of many who want to deny the historicity and physicality of the bodily resurrection, namely, to accommodate the worldview of "modern man," and we must echo Fee, that will scarcely do.

12. William Hendriksen, *The Gospel of Matthew* (Grand Rapids: Baker, 1973), 534–35.

13. See Alan G. Padgett, "Advice for Religious Historians: On the Myth of a Purely Historical Jesus," *The Resurrection,* ed. Stephen Davis, Daniel Kendall, and Gerald O'Collins, (New York: Oxford Univ. Press, 1997), 287–307.

14. Roy W. Hoover, "A Contest Between Orthodoxy and Veracity," ed. Paul Copan and Ronald K. Tacelli, *Jesus' Resurrection: Fact or Figment?: A Debate Between William Lane Craig and Gerd Lüdemann* (Downers Grove, Ill.: InterVarsity, 2000), 125. In the debate between Craig and Crossan (Paul Copan, *Will the Real Jesus Please Stand Up?: A Debate Between William Lane Craig and John Dominic Crossan* [Grand Rapids: Baker, 1998], 149), Crossan finally acknowledges the issue and impasse of incommensurate presuppositions: "It does not help to argue that one's opponents are less logical, rational, or critical than oneself, when in fact they are just as logical, rational, and critical but work from divergent presuppositions."

15. While I very much appreciate and utilize the scholarship of a Christian scholar and apologist like William Lane Craig, I have some reservations about his approach. In his debates with those who deny the Resurrection, for example, he repeatedly identifies the evidence at hand as "apostolic testimony" but does not identify the evidence as the Bible—God's Word. Yet if pressed, he probably would admit that his confidence in the evidence is grounded in his belief that the apostolic testimony of which he speaks is God's Word. Although Craig's objective in such an approach is to present the evidence in a way that is convincing to the unbeliever, he does not seem to have been successful. See Paul Copan, *Will the Real Jesus Please Stand Up?,* 59. At least one scholar, commenting on a debate between Craig and Gerd Lüedemann, has observed: "Craig's argument makes it quite clear that he is not merely 'open' to a supernaturalist worldview; he is committed to it. The result is that in his argument, historical inquiry is subservient to theological conviction." Hoover, "A Contest Between Orthodoxy and Veracity," *Jesus' Resurrection,* 127.

16. Padgett, "Advice for Religious Historians," *The Resurrection,* 287, 307.

17. Wolfhart Pannenberg, *Systematic Theology,* vol. 2 (Grand Rapids: Eerdmans, 1991), 344, cf. 344–57.

18. See Greg L. Bahnsen, *Van Til's Apologetic* (Phillipsburg, N.J.: Presbyterian & Reformed, 1998), 272 n. 30.

19. Thomas F. Torrance, *Space, Time and Resurrection* (Edinburgh: T & T Clark, 1976), 94–95.

20. D. A. Carson, "Matthew," *The Expositors Bible Commentary,* ed. Frank E. Gaebelein, vol. 8 (Grand Rapids: Zondervan, 1984), 580; "('spirit' here is equivalent to 'life')."

21. D. A. Carson, *The Gospel According to John* (Grand Rapids: Eerdmans, 1991), 623.
22. Medical explanations of this event can be found in Carson, *The Gospel According to John*, 623; and W. D. Edwards, W. J. Gabel, and F. E. Hosmer, "On the Physical Death of Jesus Christ," *Journal of the American Medical Association 255* (1986): 1455–63.
23. *Quran* Sura 4. 156–59; see also Norman L. Geisler and Abdul Saleeb, *Answering Islam: The Crescent in the Light of the Cross* (Grand Rapids: Baker, 1993), 65.
24. Hank Hanegraaff, *Resurrection* (Nashville: Nelson, 2000), 7–8. This author references another debate between William Lane Craig and a scholar who denies the Resurrection.
25. E. P. Sanders, *The Historical Figure of Jesus* (New York: Penguin, 1993), 277–78.
26. Ibid., 278.
27. Fee, *The First Epistle to the Corinthians*, 749; see Acts 26:23.
28. See Hans Conzelmann, *1 Corinthians: A Commentary on the First Epistle to the Corinthians*, ed. George W. MacRea, trans. James W. Leitch, *Hermenia* (Philadelphia: Fortress, 1975), 268.
29. Warren C. Young, "Supernatural, Supernaturalism," *Baker's Dictionary of Theology* (Grand Rapids: Baker, 1960), 507.
30. The following list is taken from Norman L. Geisler, "Resurrection, Physical Nature of," in *Baker Encyclopedia of Christian Apologetics* (Grand Rapids: Baker, 1999), 667–69; see also John F. Walvoord, *Jesus Christ Our Lord* (Chicago: Moody, 1969), 202–3. For a more extensive study, see Stephen T. Davis, *Risen Indeed: Making Sense of the Resurrection* (Grand Rapids: Eerdmans, 1993), 43–61.
31. Warfield, "The Resurrection of Christ," 195.
32. Ibid., 199.
33. J. Dwight Pentecost, *Things to Come* (Grand Rapids: Zondervan, 1958), 393.
34. See Paul Benware, *Understanding End Times Prophecy* (Chicago: Moody, 1995), 60–61; and Walvoord, *Jesus Christ Our Lord*, 217.
35. Walvoord, *Jesus Christ Our Lord*, 285–86.

Kevin D. Zuber is assistant professor of theology at the Moody Bible Institute. He earned his Ph.D. from Trinity Evangelical Divinity School, Deerfield, Illinois, and has degrees from Grace College and Grace Theological Seminary, Winona Lake, Indiana.

7

PILLAR AND GROUND OF THE TRUTH

THE CHURCH
AND ITS DOCTRINE

John Koessler

Some years ago a popular regional magazine that targeted a major American city featured a regular column devoted to reviews of local church services. Each week the columnist would attend worship at a different congregation and write a critique similar to the kind of review one might read about a movie, book, or concert. The author commented on the music, overall atmosphere of the service and, most importantly, the sermon.

To some this might have seemed a bit crass—reducing the church's worship to the level of entertainment. In reality, the reviewer only formalized the kind of evaluation being made by worshipers in these same congregations on any given Sunday.

For obvious reasons, the sermon is one of the primary things church attendees evaluate. Usually it is the sermon's style rather than its doctrine that is under scrutiny. Was the preacher interesting? Were people bored during the message? Did it seem to drag on forever? How practical was the message for daily living?

As important as these features may be to the sermon, its foundation must ultimately be a matter of doctrine. Ian Pitt-Watson, professor of preaching at Fuller Theological Seminary, underscored the twofold challenge of preaching when he observed: "Every sermon is stretched like a bow string between the text of the Bible on the one hand and the problems of contemporary human life on the other. If the string is insecurely tethered to either end, the bow is useless."[1] Even the most interesting sermon, if it lacks a basis in foundational truth, is nothing more than an exercise in tickling ears.

"It's worthless to engage people and not bring them to face God's truth," warned Graham Johnston in *Preaching to a Postmodern World,* "and likewise, it is absurd to declare to the world 'good news' with an indifference as to whether the listener responds. To lose either of these burdens results in not being heard or in having nothing to say."[2] That the preacher bears this dual burden is not surprising. The church's nature and mission demand it. What, after all, is the church? It is "the pillar and support of the truth" (1 Tim. 3:15 NASB). There is, however, a surprising order in this verse. It is the church that is described as the pillar and support and not the other way around. The church supports the truth. This means that the church has an obligation to the truth.

TRADITIONS THAT SUPPORT THE TRUTH

One might well expect this. We are saved through "belief in the truth" (2 Thess. 2:13). Those who refuse to believe the truth will be condemned (2 Thess. 2:12). In His prayer in Gethsemane, Jesus asked the Father to sanctify the church through the truth (John 17:17). It is not surprising, then, that the Scriptures emphasize the church's obligation to hand down its most central doctrines from one generation to the next. This responsibility is implied in the Scripture's use of the language of tradition when speaking of the church's teaching.

The New Testament does not view every tradition favorably. Jesus accused the religious leaders of His day of using their traditions as an excuse to disobey God's Law. As an example, He described their habit of appealing to a legal loophole that allowed grown children to avoid using their possessions to help their parents by declaring them "given to God" (Matt. 15:5; Mark 7:9–11 NASB). This practice, known as "corban," amounted to a kind of deferred giving program and involved a commitment to give something to God at a later date. In the meantime, those who had made the commitment were free to use what they had promised as their own. Jesus described a circumstance in which someone's aging parents were in need. Prompted by greed, they declared whatever might have helped the parents, either a material possession or a sum of money, to be "given to God." According to the tradition of the Pharisees and the scribes, this placed the item off-limits. Jesus pointed out that it also effectively nullified God's commands to treat one's parents with respect. Tradition, when it is used to create man-made loopholes that evade the true intent of God's commands, is a bad thing.

Like Jesus, the apostle Paul also condemned certain types of tradition. In Colossians 2:8 he warned: "See to it that no one takes you captive through hollow and deceptive philosophy, which depends on human tradition and the basic principles of this world rather than on Christ." Tradition was the basis for "hollow and deceptive philosophy," whose primary flaw was that it did not come from Christ but was of human origin. Paul, however, did not condemn all tradition. In fact he commanded the Thessalonians to "hold to the teachings" that had been passed on to them (2 Thess. 2:15). The Greek word that the *New International Version* translates "teachings" in this verse is the word for tradition. It literally meant, that which was "handed down." Similarly, Paul spoke favorably of tradition when he warned the Thessalonians to "keep away from every brother who is idle and does not live according to the teaching [literally, "tradition"] you received from us" (2 Thess. 3:6).

Scripture, then, recognizes two kinds of tradition. One is condemned, while the other is commended. The thing that separates them, ultimately, is not the manner in which they are transmitted but their source. Either kind may be handed down in oral or written form (cf. 2 Thess. 2:15). Both are passed from one generation to another. The tradition that Paul sanctioned was distinguished by the fact that it originated with God, was delivered to the apostles, and had been entrusted to the church for safekeeping and proclamation. Jude describes this same tradition as "the faith that was once for all entrusted to the saints" (Jude 3).

THEOLOGICAL UNITY
AND DOCTRINAL DIVERSITY

The faith that Jude referred to is not the Christian's experience of belief but the content of what is believed. It is *the* faith rather than personal faith that is in view. What is more, he characterized this body of doctrine as something that has been handed down to the church "once for all." This implies finality. Jude's language points to an unchanging core of theological truths that has permanent validity and does not need to be revised. This doctrinal core serves as the foundation for all theological reflection.

Paul used a different metaphor than Jude to convey the same truth, writing that the church has been "built on the foundation of the apostles and prophets" (Eph. 2:20). John Stott has noted: "Since apostles and prophets were both groups with a teaching role, it seems clear that what constitutes the church's foundation is neither their person nor their office but their instruction."[3] A foundation, once laid, does not have to be laid again and again.

All subsequent building takes place upon what has already been set in place. Moreover, it is the foundation that establishes the broad outline of what is constructed upon it. In the same way, the doctrinal core that has been entrusted to the church establishes the boundaries for its theological constructs.

Elsewhere Paul uses the metaphor of a foundation when speaking of the responsibility of those who preach and teach. According to 1 Corinthians 3:10–12, the church's one foundation is Jesus Christ. Just as the person of Christ is the cornerstone of the church, it is the doctrine of Christ that is the cornerstone of all that the church teaches.[4] However, while the foundation is fixed, the building itself is not. There is room for development, and those who build upon the one foundation need to be careful about how they build (1 Cor. 3:10).

There is a sense, then, in which the church's theology is fixed. Since the theological foundation upon which the church is built is a matter of divine revelation recorded in God's inerrant and infallible Word, it is predetermined and unchanging. It is comprised of the things that the church must believe in order to be the church. That is why these truths, sometimes referred to as "the fundamentals of the faith," comprise the *sine qua non* of the Christian faith. If any of them is missing, one no longer has true Christianity.

At the same time, the church's doctrine is also fluid to a degree. Labeling the doctrines of biblical inerrancy, the Virgin Birth, the deity of Christ, substitutionary atonement, and the bodily resurrection and return of Christ as "fundamentals" implies that there may be room for a measure of diversity on the other doctrines that do not fall into this category. Not everyone need agree on these secondary doctrines in order to properly be called a Christian, or even evangelical.

Reformed theology and dispensationalism, for example, two major theological constructs in the evangelical tradition, have both traditionally agreed on the fundamentals of the faith but have otherwise had significant differences between them. The key tenet of dispensational theology is its assertion that Israel and the church differ from each other and that God's plan for the ages re- volves around His purposes for Israel. Reformed theology, on the other hand, has tended to view Israel and the church as synony- mous with each other. For the most part, dispensationalists have held to a literal one-thousand-year reign of Christ yet in the fu- ture, while those in the Reformed tradition have held a less literal interpretation of the biblical statements regarding Christ's king- dom. These two theological systems are themselves the result of significant differences in the practice of biblical interpretation (i.e., hermeneutics). Both are human attempts to organize and un- derstand God's revealed truth. As a result, they are both neces- sarily fallible and subject to development and change. The truth upon which these two systems are based is inerrant and infalli- ble, but the theologians' efforts to interpret and categorize that truth is not.

This means that the local church has a dual responsibility when it comes to theology. It must discern between essentials and nonessentials both in doctrine and practice. At some point, every church must identify the bare minimum that must be believed be- fore it will extend "the right hand of fellowship" to another who also claims to be a Christian. At the same time, the church has the freedom to determine which "secondary" doctrines and prac- tices are important enough to its heritage and identity to require assent. It may be entirely appropriate for a particular congrega- tion to deny someone membership on the basis of its view of bap- tism, current status of the gifts of the Holy Spirit, or eschatology, as long as this does not also automatically imply that the one being refused membership is not a Christian simply because he or she has a different view on these matters.

Recognizing the difference between the fundamentals of the faith and secondary doctrines also allows the church to affirm the ideal of theological unity without requiring doctrinal uniformity.

One congregation might welcome those who hold differing views on secondary theological doctrines without feeling that they have compromised their convictions. Another congregation may make agreement on some secondary doctrine a requirement for membership but choose to engage in cooperative ministry with other congregations that hold a different view without fear of being hypocritical.

DOES DOCTRINAL DIVERSITY MEAN THEOLOGICAL RELATIVISM?

Realism demands that we acknowledge the inevitability of a certain amount of doctrinal diversity within the church. But it also raises a troubling question. Wouldn't doctrinal uniformity be better for the church's witness? More importantly, isn't doctrinal agreement something that God desires from the church? Tolerating a variety of theological views on nonessentials smacks of theological relativism. Such a practice could imply that all doctrinal positions, even those that are mutually contradictory, are equally valid.

The Purpose: Seeking Unity

Clearly Jesus' purpose for the church was that it would experience unity. He promised that His church would be "one flock and one shepherd" (John 10:16). He prayed for His followers and asked that "all of them may be one" (John 17:21). Likewise, the apostle Paul urged the Ephesian church to "make every effort to keep the unity of the Spirit through the bond of peace" (Eph. 4:3). He spoke of one body, one Spirit, one hope, one faith, one baptism, and one God and Father over all (Eph. 4:4–6). The Scriptures make it equally clear, however, that the perfect unity for which Jesus prayed will not become a reality until the end of the age (1 Cor. 13:10). Ephesians 4:11–12 notes that God has provided apostles, prophets, evangelists, and pastor/teachers to move the church in the direction of doctrinal unity but acknowledges that their ministry will continue "until we all reach unity in the faith and in the knowledge of the Son of God and become mature, attaining to the whole measure of the fullness of Christ" (v. 13).

Although some of the ministries listed by Paul in these verses appear to have been foundational in nature and limited to the New Testament era (cf. Eph. 2:20), the ongoing validity of the ministry of evangelists, pastors, and teachers is beyond dispute. In other words, as long as there are evangelists, pastors, and teachers serving the church, we can be certain that it has not yet achieved the unity of knowledge and truth spoken of here. In the meantime, we are in the process of growth and development. What we know, we know only "in part" and what we understand we understand imperfectly (1 Cor. 13:12). It is our own weakness and imperfection that requires that we tolerate a measure of doctrinal diversity.

The Practice: Finding a Healthy Balance

The apostle Paul's counsel to the Corinthians regarding the New Testament practice of eating meat sacrificed to idols provides the church with a model of healthy balance in dealing with theological diversity. Some New Testament believers were able to eat meat that had been sacrificed to idols without feeling any guilt because they recognized the theological truth that "an idol is nothing" and that there is "no God but one" (1 Cor. 8:4). Others, because of their past experience with pagan worship, viewed the same meat as defiled (v. 7). Although Paul admitted that those who felt the freedom to eat had the "right" theology, he counseled them to accommodate those who did not share that same liberty (vv. 11–13). The net effect of such an approach meant that the Corinthian church had members with differing theological convictions about the same practice.

However, while Paul was tolerant of doctrinal diversity in this matter, he did not endorse theological relativism. If there was a relativistic dimension to the problem, it was limited to the practice of eating, not the theology behind it. He allowed different convictions and practices to coexist, but he made it clear that both views could not be right. The idol could not be something and nothing at the same time. The idol was nothing (1 Cor. 8:4). There could not be both one God and many gods. The weaker believer's sin when eating was due to his acting against his conscience, not to the nature of the idol itself.

Paul's ability to affirm a single theological truth while tolerating multiple views in the same congregation is a reminder that tolerating doctrinal diversity is not the same thing as saying that everyone's theology is correct. A church can acknowledge that "good men disagree" on an issue without implying that every view is equally valid. It can identify itself with a doctrinal distinctive or theological system and still be true to the Scripture's call to unity in the body of Christ by making a distinction between the fundamentals of the faith and secondary doctrines.

WORSHIP AS A THEOLOGICAL EXERCISE

The church's theological stewardship obviously affects its ministry of teaching. What may be less recognized is the bearing that it has on the church's ministry of worship. Ultimately, worship is a theological exercise. This is implied in the command of Colossians 3:16 to "let the word of Christ dwell in you richly as you teach and admonish one another with all wisdom, and as you sing psalms, hymns and spiritual songs with gratitude in your hearts to God."

A Focus on Theological Content

Interestingly, Paul did not commend worship for how it makes believers feel towards God but for what it teaches about Him. He described worship as a means of instruction. H. C. G. Moule observed, "The spiritual importance of Christian hymnody comes out impressively here. It is no mere luxury of devotion, certainly no mere musical pleasure; it is an ordained vehicle of instruction and warning."[5] Worship is the handmaid of doctrine. It should convey theological content.

This is significant, in view of the contemporary church's tendency to view worship as synonymous with music. This perspective is reflected in the common practice of designating the portion of the service where hymns or choruses are sung as "worship," implying that congregational worship ends when the sermon begins. The church's habit of viewing worship as identical with musical expression is especially reflected in congregational conflicts over "worship," which usually focus more on musical style than on content.

Interestingly, the New Testament has virtually nothing to say about worship style. The few glimpses that it does offer of the early church's habits of worship provide little in the way of detailed information about their practices. We know that music played a part but learn nothing about the kind of music the congregants preferred. It seems reasonable to assume that the style reflected the culture. Jewish congregations probably worshiped in a style reminiscent of the synagogue. Gentile congregations may have used other forms. We do not really know. Did they use musical instruments to accompany their worship? What was the proportion of singing compared to the amount of time devoted to listening to the sermon? Did they limit themselves to congregational singing or did they listen to solos? The Scriptures do not say.

Worship in the Early Church

The description of congregational life in Acts 2:42 paints a picture in broad strokes and mentions only four things: teaching, fellowship, the breaking of bread (possibly a reference to communion), and prayer. The apostle Paul provided a little more detail when he described Corinthian worship as so participatory that church members were vying with one another for attention: "What then shall we say, brothers? When you come together, everyone has a hymn, or a word of instruction, a revelation, a tongue or an interpretation. All of these must be done for the strengthening of the church" (1 Cor. 14:26). Although Paul mentions hymns, the primary emphasis in Corinthian worship was on teaching and forms of divine revelation. In other words, it was focused primarily on God's Word.

Extrabiblical writing sheds little additional light on the question of how the early church worshiped. The earliest description of congregational worship to be found outside the New Testament is the account of Pliny the Younger in his letter to the emperor Trajan (c. A.D. 112). Writing from Bithynia, Pliny asked for instruction in how to deal with the new sect known as Christians. He said that it was their practice "to meet before daybreak, and to recite a hymn antiphonally to Christ as to a god, and to bind themselves by an oath [sacramentum], not for the commission of any crime but to abstain from theft, robbery, adultery, breach of faith, and not to deny a deposit when claimed."[6] Pliny added that these believers met again later in the day to share a common meal. Tertullian, writing about eighty years later, described his congregation: "We meet together as an assembly and congregation, that, offering up prayer to God as with united force, we may wrestle with Him in our supplications."[7]

In addition, early congregational worship included the public reading of Scripture and exhortation. Once a month, members in Tertullian's congregation gave an offering that was used to help bury the poor, care for orphans, and supply the needs of the elderly. The atmosphere, according to Tertullian, was one of gravity, "as befits those who feel assured that they are in the sight of God."[8] After sharing a common meal, the congregation listened as individual believers sang hymns, either drawn from the Scriptures or of their own composition.

Paul's categories of psalms, hymns, and spiritual songs in Colossians 3:16 (also found in Eph. 5:19) indicate that congregational worship in the New Testament era employed a variety of forms. His chief concern, however, was not with the particular form or certain style but with the content of worship. Whether it took the form of a psalm, hymn, or spiritual song, worship was to express "the Word of Christ." Contrast this with the practice of the church today, which tends to gauge its worship almost exclusively on the basis of how it makes the worshiper feel. The affective dimension is far more important than the theological.

Perhaps the vagueness of the New Testament on the subject of the church's worship is intentional. God's purpose spans the ages and incorporates a multitude of cultures. A single style or form could not possibly serve such a vast audience. Yet one of the New Testament's few statements about this subject makes it clear that God does have a standard by which He judges the church's worship. After an extended discussion about theology and worship, Jesus told the woman of Samaria that the Father was seeking a certain kind of worshiper. "God is spirit," He declared, "and his worshipers must worship in spirit and in truth" (John 4:24). Spirit and truth are the two great poles that define the landscape of worship for the church. Sincerity alone is not enough. Enthusiasm is good but may be misdirected. Faith is essential but must be fixed on the right object. True worship, as Christ defined it, is an exercise of the heart guided by the truth.

It is time for the church to declare a truce in the worship wars and adopt a more objective standard for evaluating its worship. Let the church subject its various styles and forms to the test

of theology rather than of taste. What it says is far more important than how it sounds. What does it say about God's nature?
What does it say about God's purpose? Most important of all,
what does it say about Christ?

THE CENTRALITY OF CHRIST

This last question points to one of the most notable features
of the list of truths commonly known as the fundamentals of
the faith. It is one-sided. As important as it is to the life and faith
of the church, it does not cover all the categories of systematic
theology. Its topics are primarily drawn from the sphere of Christology. This is not surprising given the historical context of the
fundamentalist movement. Early fundamentalism was responding to a devastating shift away from biblical orthodoxy to theological liberalism, one of whose central features was a denial of
Christ's nature and work. The early fundamentalists, like the early church, correctly understood that the viability and authenticity of the Christian faith stands or falls on its view of Christ. It
is not simply theology but Christian theology—Christ-centered
theology—that the church believes and teaches.

The centrality of Christ is also the dominant theological truth
that orders the practice of the church. Paul emphasized the centrality of Christ to the church when he called Him the "head"
of the church (Eph. 4:15; Col. 1:18; 2:10, 19). This metaphor had
a twofold emphasis. It spoke of Christ as the church's ultimate
authority and as its source.[9] That Paul understood Christ's headship in an authoritative sense is clear from the practical applications he made when using this metaphor. For example, when he
addressed the practices of public prayer and prophecy in the
church of Corinth, Paul commanded men and women to pray and
prophesy in a way that symbolized divinely ordered authority.
In the Corinthian context, this meant either wearing a head
covering or praying and prophesying with one's head bare. Men

were to pray and prophesy with their heads uncovered. A man who did so with a covered head "dishonored" his head (1 Cor. 11:4). On the other hand, it would have been equally disgraceful for a woman to pray without her head covered. Paul characterized the woman's head covering as a "sign of authority" (1 Cor. 11:10). Although there may have been some cultural factors that prompted the command, ultimately he grounded it in the headship of Christ, introducing both stipulations with the statement: "Now I want you to realize that the head of every man is Christ, and the head of the woman is man, and the head of Christ is God" (1 Cor. 11:3).

Paul used a similar line of reasoning when he called believing wives to submit to the authority of their husbands, basing his appeal on Christ's headship of the church: "Wives, submit to your husbands as to the Lord. For the husband is the head of the wife as Christ is the head of the church, his body, of which he is the Savior" (Eph. 5:22–23).

Paul also appealed to the headship of Christ when he warned the Colossians of the danger of allowing "false humility and the worship of angels" to displace Christ as the focus of the church's worship and practice (Col. 2:18–19). Elsewhere, Paul urged believers to practice humility, the essence of which was to regard others as more important than oneself (Phil. 2:3). The condemnation in Colossians 2:18–19 was not aimed at this kind of true humility but was directed at sham humility. In the Colossian context, this took the form of dietary laws, summarized by the three stipulations: "Do not handle! Do not taste! Do not touch!" (Col. 2:21).

This was the kind of religion practiced by the Pharisees and condemned by Jesus, an approach to worship and the spiritual life that was more concerned with appearance than with the heart (Luke 11:39–42). Those condemned by Paul also engaged in angel worship. Jewish thought in Paul's day was given to unhealthy speculation about angels. For some, this interest spilled over into outright worship. The author of the book of Hebrews also addressed this problem and took pains to prove to his readers that Jesus was far superior to the angels (Heb. 1:1–2:3). Authority lay at the heart of such practices, since those who engaged in them believed that they were subject to spiritual forces and were bound by decrees like those found in the Law of Moses (Col. 2:16–20). Paul reminded these misguided worshipers that their habits of devotion were to be governed by a higher standard: "Since, then, you have been raised with Christ, set your hearts on things above, where Christ is seated at the right hand of God. Set your minds on things above, not on earthly things. For you died, and your life is now hidden with Christ in God" (Col. 3:1–3).

PRACTICAL IMPLICATIONS FOR THE CHURCH

As its "head," Christ alone can define the church's mission (Matt. 28:18–20; John 20:21). This is a needed corrective in an age of market-driven ministry. There is no disputing the church's need to be sensitive to its cultural context. The apostle Paul understood this and planted churches with a philosophy of ministry that he summarized as one of becoming "all things to all men" (1 Cor. 9:22). This approach, however, was limited. Culture may have played a role in determining his methods, but it did not define the aim of his ministry. That agenda had already been established for him. It was to proclaim and teach Christ in order to "present everyone perfect in Christ" (Col. 1:28). It was not primarily to transform the culture by working for social justice, although that was often a by-product of preaching Christ. Nor was it primarily to improve the individual's moral behavior, although that was also one of the inevitable results of carrying out the church's mission. Paul's goal was to preach Christ, to worship Christ, and to see Christ's transforming power reflected in the lives of those who had believed in Christ as a result of his ministry.

Paul was sensitive to the "market" without being market

driven. An approach to ministry that is culturally sensitive adapts its ministry structures in the hope that it will be able to incorporate others into the church and bring them to the place where they will submit to Christ's purpose for their lives. It is flexible, but it is not entirely "free." It is not under the law but is under Christ's authority (1 Cor. 9:21). Consequently, the church has freedom but does not have the liberty to exceed the boundaries set for it by God's Word. For the Reformers, this meant that church life as well as one's personal life should be governed by the rule of *sola scriptura* (Scripture alone). John Calvin observed that one aspect of the fear of God "consists simply in worshiping him as he commands, mingling no inventions of our own."[10] Consequently, the church's practice is marked by form as well as freedom. The ultimate authority to determine what constitutes acceptable worship does not rest with the personal tastes of the unchurched, the congregation, or even the church's leaders but with the Scriptures.

When Paul called Christ the head of the church, he also implied something about the nature of the church itself. It is both a living organism and an organization. It enjoys a mystical communion with Christ and with all its members, but it also lives with the reality of a structure of leadership. Christ is its only head, but it is served by elders and deacons (1 Tim. 3:1–9; 4:14; 5:17; Phil. 1:1). Furthermore, a head necessarily implies a body made up of many members, each with its own distinct function but all of them working together for the common good. This is precisely how Paul described the nature of the church in its relation to Christ: "The body is a unit, though it is made up of many parts; and though all its parts are many, they form one body. So it is with Christ" (1 Cor. 12:12).

Depending on Christ in Diverse Worship Settings

The individual members perform a variety of functions, each one placed there by the sovereign purpose of God's Spirit. The one body of Christ is made up of many congregations, and each congregation in turn contains many members. They work toward the same purpose and are empowered by the same Spirit, but they do not look the same. Each congregation has its own unique ministry environment and collection of spiritual gifts. They differ in size, in age, in style, and often in methodology.

The fact that the Scriptures can speak of one church and many churches at the same time is a signal that the local church experiences unity within a context of individual congregational diversity (Matt. 16:18; John 10:16; Acts 15:41; Rom. 16:3–5). Churches do not all have to be the same in order to be "biblical." There is room for a variety of sizes and styles. The differences between them are primarily a result of differences in ministry context and the Holy Spirit's sovereign distribution of gifts and resources (1 Cor. 12:18). All are engaged in the same common task and depend upon the same God for success. They are not competitors who need to beat out the others for their "market share."

Consequently, acknowledging Christ as its head means that the church will exercise its ministry with a sense of its dependency upon Christ. It is the head that empowers and directs the rest of the body. Those who have been joined to Christ by faith recognize that Christ has empowered them to live a new life. Their awareness of His imminent return determines their values and their priorities, while the knowledge that they have died and risen with Christ shapes their moral choices and gives them the confidence that their ministry will be marked by God's power (Col. 3:3–5). New Testament scholar F. F. Bruce explained: "Their life is the life of Christ, maintained by Him with all His people. Their interests must therefore be His interests. Instead of waiting until the last day to receive the resurrection-life, those who have been raised with Christ possess it in the here and now."[11]

This means that those who are already a part of the church, as well as the unchurched, have a right to expect the church to be more than a merely human institution. It is true that the church is not yet perfect, but it should be different. Perhaps the magazine editor who decided that congregational life merited review and public comment was not so far off the mark after all. The congregation whose ambition rises no higher than a civic organization, whose lifestyle is no different from the unchurched, and whose preaching has no more power than the typical motivational speaker has fallen from Christ's true intent. It has forgotten that it follows in the steps of the church that once caused an unbelieving world to marvel at its life and message and declare, "See how they love one another!" [12]

Returning to the Fundamentals

This obligation brings us, inevitably, back to the fundamentals. Despite its best intentions, the church can rise no higher than what it believes. This is so for the simple reason that the church's experience cannot go beyond the truth—that which is true about itself and is true about Christ. Moreover, these two are intimately connected. What is true of the church is so because of the truth about Christ.

One practical implication of this is the responsibility that it lays upon the church to preserve and protect the fundamental truths that have been entrusted to its care. This is what Jude meant when he urged his readers to "contend" for the faith (Jude 3). The truth "that was once for all entrusted to the church" has been subject to attack and distortion ever since it was first revealed. Furthermore, Scripture warns that assaults upon the church's doctrinal foundation will not only continue, but those assaults will actually increase as the day of Christ's return draws near (2 Tim. 4:3). One of the church's most important tasks, then, is its role as a caretaker of the truth. Timothy George used the language of stewardship to describe this responsibility when he wrote, "Theologians are not freelance scholars of religion, but trustees of the deposit of faith that they, like pastors, are charged with passing on intact to the rising generation."[13]

By emphasizing the theologian's pastoral responsibility, however, George has inadvertently drawn a distinction between the pastor and the theologian. Whether or not he actually meant to do so, it must be admitted that this dichotomy is one that is reflected in the life of the church and its training institutions. It is a false and dangerous distinction. During the fundamentalist/modernist struggle of the nineteenth century, some of the most critical battles were fought in the church's theological training institutions, precisely because evangelical leaders of that era correctly understood the link between the pulpit and the pew in shaping the church's theology.

The struggle continues today but on a somewhat different field of battle. In some Bible colleges and seminaries, for example, it is not unusual to find students divided between those who are being trained for pastoral ministry and those who are being trained to teach theology. The former track is often seen as "practical" while the latter is viewed as "theological." This distinction is fed by alumni who complain, often with reason, that their training was not practical enough and never really taught them how to "be" a pastor. The most popular books in the field are written by motivational speakers reducing pastoral theology to the "soft science" of evangelicalism. Too many of the texts read by future pastors have more in common with social sciences than with the "queen of sciences."

The pastor's theological calling has been further undermined by evangelicalism's predominate culture of pragmatism. Evangelical churches, denominations, and training institutions have begun recommending that their pastors adopt new role models for their ministry. The theologian has been replaced by the therapist and the entrepreneur.[14]

It is time for pastors to reclaim the theologian's mantle. Every theologian need not be a pastor, but every pastor must be a theologian. When it comes to the task of passing on the church's deposit of faith to the "rising generation," it is the pastor, not the theologian, who stands on the front lines. In the end it will be the theology of the pulpit that will determine the doctrine of the pew.

NOTES

1. Ian Pitt-Watson, cited by John Stott in *Between Two Worlds: The Art of Preaching in the Twentieth Century* (Grand Rapids: Eerdmans, 1982), 150.
2. Graham Johnston, *Preaching to a Postmodern World* (Grand Rapids: Baker, 2001), 19.
3. John Stott, *God's New Society: The Message of Ephesians* (Downers Grove, Ill.: InterVarsity, 1979), 106–7.
4. Charles Hodge's comment regarding 1 Corinthians 4:11 is helpful: "This may be understood either of the person or the doctrine of Christ. In either way the sense is good. Christ, as the incarnate Son of God, according to one Scriptural figure, is the head of the church which is his body, that is he is the source of its life; according to another figure, he is its foundation or cornerstone, because on him all the members of the church, considered as a temple rest for salvation. On the other hand, however, it is also true that the doctrine concerning Christ is the fundamental doctrine of the gospel. We may, therefore, understand the apostle to say, that the work of the ministry is to build up the church on the foundation which *God* has laid in the person and work of Christ. There can be no other ground of confidence for justification, sanctification, and salvation of men. Or we may understand him to say, that the work of those who followed him in Corinth was simply to build on the foundation which *he* had laid, in preaching the doctrine of Christ crucified, for there can be no other foundation of the church than that doctrine." *A Commentary on 1 & 2 Corinthians* (1857; reprint, Carlisle, Pa.: Banner of Truth Trust, 1974), 55.
5. H. C. G. Moule, *Studies in Colossians and Philemon* (1893; reprint, Grand Rapids: Kregel, 1977), 129.
6. Henry Bettenson, *Documents of the Christian Church* (London: Oxford, 1963), 4–5.
7. Tertullian, *Apology XXXIX, The Ante-Nicene Fathers*, ed. Alexander Roberts and James Donaldson, vol. 3 (Grand Rapids: Eerdmans, 1976), 46.
8. Ibid.
9. Thomas R. Schreiner, *Paul, Apostle of God's Glory in Christ* (Downers Grove, Ill.: InterVarsity, 2001), 337–38.
10. John Calvin, *The Institutes of the Christian Religion*, (4.10.23), ed. John T. McNeill, trans. Ford Lewis Battles, vol. 2 (Philadelphia: Westminster, 1977), 1202.
11. E. K. Simpson and F. F. Bruce, *Commentary on the Epistles to the Ephesians and Colossians* (Grand Rapids: Eerdmans, 1979), 259.
12. Tertullian, *Apology,* 46.
13. Timothy George, "A Theology to Die For," *Christianity Today,* 9 February 1998, 49.

14. Bruce Shelley suggests that models for pastoral ministry have shifted from the pastor/theologian to the professional minister to that of the enterprising healer. Bruce L. Shelley, "The Seminary's Identity Crisis," *Christianity Today,* 17 May 1993, 42–44.

John Koessler is chairman and professor of the pastoral studies department at the Moody Bible Institute. He has earned a D.Min. degree from Trinity Evangelical Divinity School, Deerfield, Illinois, and has degrees from Wayne State University, Detroit, and Biblical Theological Seminary, Hatfield, Pennsylvania. Dr. Koessler is the author of six books.

8

PRECIOUS LIVING TRUTHS
FAITH AND PRACTICE IN
THE TWENTY-FIRST CENTURY

Michael McDuffee

The foundational truths of Christianity are crucial to a world-view that is based upon sound biblical theology. A Christian worldview orders our biblical thinking about how the world works. But right thinking must be coupled with a Christian ethos—our feelings about living in this world. Those feelings spring from our living relationship with our Lord. The two are inseparable. Even when we divide them as subjects of study, we can never truly separate them from each other.

These two realms of faith, the cognitive and the experiential—theology and practice—are not exclusive to evangelical Christianity. Our heritage, however, joins them in a unique way. We are descendants of both confessional Protestantism and pietism.

Reform and renewal are both characteristics of evangelical Christianity.

THE GOAL OF THEOLOGICAL REFLECTION

Every generation engages in theological reflection within the context of its own unique moment in Christian history as it moves toward the consummation of all things in Christ (Eph. 1:10). We do not hold precious truths about the story of Jesus impassively. With the knowledge that Christ is in our midst, we weep and worship, we pray and celebrate, we sing and yearn, and we study and serve! In that context we do the work of theology. One of the goals of our reflection is to teach and transmit the truths of biblical Christianity to new generations of Christians, who come out of a world held hostage to many false hopes that are in a constant state of flux. Thus theology instructs and guides church leaders in practicing pastoral care. It helps missionaries to tell the truths of Christianity to a world in need of the forgiveness of sins. Theology trains the church in how best to examine and test the claims made by others about the story of Jesus or about how one may be healed from the effects of sin.

Theology therefore serves the work of pastoral care, missions, and apologetics. It also builds up the body of Christ through the training of each believer, so that he or she may walk in the truth with love.

In all of these things, the fundamentals of the faith serve as touchstones. We refer to and rely upon them in our effort to remain loyal to the biblical tradition that has been handed down to us. We should not think that we merely deliver these great and essential truths like crated freight to new cultural territories or new periods of history. The telling, the teaching, the transmitting of biblical truth, and the testing of claims about these truths is a dynamic undertaking. Like the social world in which we live, we evangelical Christians are subject to forces of constant change.

It is the fundamentals of the faith that enable us to maintain our identity in Christ and help us to know what and how we should communicate to others. We survey the cultural landscape in order to build a doctrinal understanding of Christ which both preserves the truths of Scriptures and stimulates effective and loving Christian proclamation. We are not mere keepers of the gate or watchmen only. We are craftsmen—called to be skilled in handling accurately the Word of truth and in analyzing our times so that we might be useful to the Lord in the building of His church (2 Tim. 2:15).

These five fundamental truths of the Christian faith—biblical authority, the Virgin Birth, the deity of Christ, substitutionary atonement, and the bodily resurrection and physical return of Christ—are to guide the church in its ministries of missions, apologetics, and pastoral care. The preceding chapters have attempted to show the continued value of these doctrines. These truths help us to be steadfast in our confession of Jesus as Lord and to abide in His Word (John 8:31–32; 15:7). Jesus sanctified Himself for the sake of His apostles. He prayed for us too, that we may also be sanctified, who believe in Him through apostolic preaching (John 17:17–20). To remain loyal to our Lord Jesus, we must subject ourselves to the authority of apostolic ministry. It is our fellowship with apostolic tradition, preserved for us in the Scripture, that assures our abiding in God's Word.

WHAT IT MEANS TO BE EVANGELICAL

We are a people with a special habit, or discipline, of the faith. We make disciples of Christ among the nations by preaching the gospel and sharing our faith personally with others. Like the Gerasene demoniac, we long to tell others how much the Lord has done for us, and how He has had mercy on us (Mark 5:19). Everything we do is influenced by our desire to tell others the story of Jesus and to show them that in His name they may receive forgiveness of sins. That is what it means to be "evangelical." This emphasis upon the work of evangelism and discipleship is the badge of evangelical Christianity. The Christian man or woman who thinks evangelically confesses that God's offer of salvation to the world is the truth that lies at the heart of the Bible. God sent Jesus to give the world a Savior (John 3:17). In the same way, God sends us to share this Good News with others. We ask our neighbors, our friends, our family members, and perfect strangers, "Are you saved?" We preach the Good News, announcing what God has done for us sinners through His Son and what He requires of us for our salvation according to the Scriptures.

The gospel is our norm, in which our rule of faith is grounded. We embrace the first ecumenical council held in Jerusalem at which the apostle Peter bore witness that God would have all peoples "hear the word of the gospel and believe" (Acts 15:7 NASB).

The fundamentals of the faith define our theological paradigm with its emphasis upon redemptive history. This is an Athanasian paradigm—God alone is able to save! It is Cappadocian—only that which He has assumed is healed. It is Tertullian—baptism brings blessing through obedience for believers. It is Augustinian—we are saved through the grace of the Lord Jesus. It is Celtic, with its strong commitment to the study and dispersing of the Scriptures.

Such is catholic and orthodox Christian thinking. We embody Protestantism only to voice objection to this fundamental place of salvation being replaced by *any* tradition of men. Our theological hands are callous from working with the grain of the Reformation, which we recognize as a universal movement restoring a biblical basis to the message of salvation within the *entire* body of Christ. On the basis of Scripture we affirm a sinner receives forgiveness of sins by faith alone in the person and work of Jesus Christ our Lord.

THE EVANGELICAL FOCUS:
EVANGELISM AND THE SCRIPTURES

Beyond this, however, evangelical Christianity serves in the capacity of a subculture for renewal within the church. We continue the impulse of revival and persist in the call to Spirit-filled holy living that reaches beyond the borders of any given institutional order or particular denomination. Evangelicalism is a relatively young movement within Christianity. Because of this, we practice a kind of ecumenicity with the past by being eclectic inheritors of a spiritual legacy that stretches back for centuries. But in all that we collect and accept, we hold fast to the confession that "scripture [as the authoritative source for] the gospel, the original Christian message, must be the primary, fundamental and permanently binding criterion of any Christian theology."[1]

To this criterion we subject ourselves. Part of what it means to be an evangelical Christian is to remind the universal, visible church of this crucial key to doing the work of theology. We must be clear about two things. *First, this is our identity.* The evangelical community of Christian faith is committed to preaching the gospel to all creation. We cannot remain who we are if we forsake this. *Second, this emphasis does not absolve us of other vital activities.* We should involve ourselves in seeking social justice, pursuing the common good, and exploring matters of cultural life. But we should do these things while remaining evangelical Christians. In the pulpit and on the streets, with permission and without it, in season and out of season, the hallmark of our evangelical heritage is to preach the Word. We make no claim to this being our exclusive domain, but this is what we do, and we must do it well.

Above all else, then, to be evangelical means that we are people committed to the Scriptures. The truths contained in Scripture supply us with a compass that guides our telling, teaching, and transmitting to others the wonderful story of Jesus. We bring the Scriptures with us in our missionary, apologetic, and pastoral endeavors. We plant and build churches based upon its content. As we preach, we urge others to learn of Jesus and all matters of life, death, truth, and faith by turning to the Scriptures.

Teaching the Scriptures to others and urging them to recognize the Bible's accuracy and authority is an exercise in godly empowerment. The Scriptures, after all, provide people with a way of being liberated from selfish ambition; they show people the path to a new way of life that is pleasing to the Lord. This means that one of the church's most important responsibilities is that of teaching others how to study and understand the Scriptures themselves.

There is, of course, a risk in this. It is the risk that we might get tangled up in empty chatter and ignorant speculations. But love takes that risk. Evangelical Christianity is committed to expanding the base of global literacy and is likewise committed to the task of teaching principles of biblical interpretation and textual criticism. We do all of this while holding onto the fundamental truth that the Scriptures are authoritative and reliable. As we preach, we let people know that the sacred writings are able to give them the wisdom that leads to salvation through faith, which is in Christ Jesus (2 Tim. 3:15). We live in a time in which the forces of globalization and postmodernism have an enormous impact on peoples' lives and their futures. In a day in which we know many things yet are unsure about almost everything, only the gift of Scripture can grant us the certainty we desire.

THE DE-CHRISTIANIZATION
OF WESTERN CULTURE

The deepest longing of human experience is the desire for eternal prosperity.[2] Human communities attempt to transcend the dread of personal insignificance and the fear of death by finding meaning in life through some larger scheme into which they can fit their ancestors, themselves, and their children. We call the result of their efforts culture. All cultures carry a faint memory of the human family's divine deliverance through the Flood, and they experience the trauma of suffering divine rebuke for the Tower of Babel. As evangelical Christians, we should realize that whether implicitly or explicitly, in the hearts and minds of its members, a people's culture itself is sacred, since *it* is the "religion" that assures in some way their remaining vital and accepted by an approving authority.

Based upon these universal historical facts, religion is the heart, source, and end of all culture. Myth, as a dimension of religion, provides people with a story about how they originated, why they are important, and what they are to do with their lives. Myths serve the purpose of ordering the collective life of a people. They give the reason that people suppress certain desires, subject themselves to certain tasks, and make great sacrifices in attempting to accomplish them. Myth, then, is an "all-encompassing, activating image: a sort of vision of desirable objectives that have lost their material, practical character and have become strongly colored, overwhelming, all-encompassing and which displace from the conscious all that is related to it. Such an image pushes man to action precisely because it includes all that he feels is good, just, and true."[3]

Secularization is the primary myth of the modern Western world. Secularization is the loss of religious significance in daily life and for daily life. In a secular society, religious institutions suffer a loss of social significance and public authority. They are subsidized less by a society's most scarce resources—wealth, intellectual investment, and expenditure of time. The lessening of the Christian worldview is a particular example of this process. De-Christianization has occurred, and its effects upon the modern Western mind are undeniable.

Since the Carolingian era (ninth century), inhabitants of Western civilization have had a sense of identity and self-assurance that has been rooted in their perception of themselves as Christians and in the knowledge that others see them as such. In short, what we today call the West once knew itself as a social order of Christendom. The *Song of Roland*, the Crusades, the age of discovery, the Renaissance and Reformation, the scientific revolution, the age of revolution and romanticism, the age of progress and Western imperialism, and even the world wars of the twentieth century all grew from this same taproot. All are variations from the outgrowth of one cultural life that had as its defining nucleus the person of Jesus Christ proclaimed and worshiped by the church.

Western civilization is the fruit of Western or Latin Christendom that developed after the establishment of the Holy Roman Empire under Charles the Great. This civilization understood itself as being apart from and in opposition to both Eastern Christianity and Islam. It was a civilization that held Judaism at a distance, even at times as hostage, even though Jews contributed to its many significant and rich achievements.

The United States is an extension of this legacy with its own set of values rooted in this common Christianized heritage. The practice of civil religion in America, for example, with its emphasis upon separation of church and state, is an innovative institution in comparison to the place and role of the established church in modern Europe.

THE EFFECT OF A
DE-CHRISTIANIZED CULTURE

The effect of de-Christianization is that it convinces people to divest Christ of His role as a figure of religious power and authority. Such "deconverted" Christian consciousness sees Christ as having no legitimate right to compel obedience. It causes people to dismiss those who follow Him as well meaning but wrong. The de-Christianized majority in the West is content to be ignorant of Christ's promises and disobedient to His commands. If they are familiar with His promises and commands at all, it is a familiarity lacking in either desire or fear.

Nevertheless, the forces of de-Christianization have not been completely successful. A minority still remembers His name. Counted among this minority, evangelical Christians preach the gospel and seek to build Bible-based churches in this de-Christianized context.

De-Christianized secularization has increased the power and influence of science over our lives. Society suffers no vacuum. As religious influence has moved out of the public arena and has become increasingly restricted to the realm of personal preference, science has taken on the role of resident expert with respect to the kind of society in which we should live and how we should live in it. What is of prime importance is the choice between the pride of scientists,[4] who believe they know with absolute certainty that man is merely a part of nature, and the humble rejection of this premise. This pride has hardened into a dangerous presumption that all of life may be understood in accordance with the principles of science.

How vainglorious science truly is and, consequently, how religious it has become, is made clear by considering the following. Physicist Stephen Hawking and others have attempted to conceive of the "theory of everything," while science writer John Horgan has conceded that there were "perhaps two outstanding fundamental problems in science—immortality and consciousness"! E. O. Wilson, the great sociobiologist, believes that "one day science will be able to 'explain' art, religion, ethics, kinship patterns, forms of government, etiquette, fashion, courtship, gift-giving patterns, funeral rites, population policy, penal sanctions, and if that's not enough, virtually everything else."[5]

Today there is a growing concern that the window of opportunity for us to correct scientific arrogance and thus ensure our own survival "as a species" may be rapidly closing. The highly regarded historian Francis Fukuyama wrote recently,

The most significant threat posed by contemporary biotechnology is the possibility that it will alter human nature and thereby move us into a "posthuman" stage of history. That is important, because human nature exists, is a meaningful concept, and has provided a stable continuity to our experience as a species. It is, conjointly with religion, what defines our most basic values.[6]

As evangelicals, we should take up the task of rediscovering and examining the Christian roots of Western culture. We should be among the vanguard that communicates to others that the most "revolutionary process of the last thousand years [has been] bound up with the unification of thought [brought about] by the common possession of the Bible."[7] As evangelicals, we should assume responsibility for proclaiming this truth. But are we ourselves convinced? Or have we been conditioned too by the hollow claims of secularized academic rhetoric that has censored the past and thus buried the achievements of Christianity in the West, while its many shortcomings have been highlighted and distorted for the sake of ideology? Evangelical Christians should work to restore a more balanced assessment of the relationship between Christianity and Western culture.

EVANGELICALS IN A GLOBALIZED SOCIETY

To maintain our own equilibrium in this undertaking, we need the ballast of the fundamental truths of our faith, which the Lord has given us through the Scriptures. They will help us in our efforts to create a peaceful context, which will allow people of different allegiances and loyalties to join together to listen and learn about the life of the church in Western culture and beyond. This task is important because we have become a global culture.

The Fundamental Influence of Globalization

Globalization, the fundamental influence in our lives today, has reduced the social distance between peoples of different cultures. Globalization is the close proximity of diverse communities. People of different cultures encounter one another more often and in more ways than ever before. But this means far more than just meeting more people who are different from us. It affects how we understand truth and how we gain our sense of certainty.

Globalization is a "social process in which the constraints of geography on social and cultural arrangements recede *and in which people become increasingly aware that they are receding*"[8] (emphasis added). Globalization, of course, has great impact on economic and political activities. It transforms production practices and the nature of political authority. Profit and power often seem to be dispersed, when in actuality they are becoming more concentrated. Globalization's greatest impact, however, is on our sense of cultural orientation and our sense of social identity. It alters social arrangements and the allocation of scarce resources "for the production, exchange and expression of symbols that represent facts, affects, meanings, beliefs, preferences, tastes and values."[9]

In summary, globalization is in the business of creating new myths. Evangelical Christians need the fundamentals of the faith to develop a theology that will expose the falsehood of the new global myths that are being born today.

Whatever form these new myths take, the wounds society suffers from will be the same as those of our common fallen past. Global change will continue to leave in its wake familiar problems in a new arrangement of global jealousy, fear, envy, anger, and hatred. The desires of the flesh will continue to plague the soul of the new globalized man, just as it did the men and women of the ancient world. The older secular political religions of the twentieth century—liberalism, Marxism, fascism—will not have the power to call and to convert men and women to a common goal. The old ideologies are fallen gods. In their place, the reigning gods of science and globalization, of market and media are producing people in their own image. Yet neither science nor politics can deal with the universal problems of guilt, resentment, remorse, and indignation. A very old story will continue to be lived out on a new kind of stage.

Evangelical Christians will need to be well grounded in the Scriptures if they are to bring the good news of Jesus to this strange new world.

The Resurgence of Religion

During the foreseeable future, a revitalized religion, led by a resurgent Islam, will shape the global culture.[10] For more than a generation now, we have witnessed a resurgence of religious life throughout the world. Historians and social scientists have used such cumbersome terms as "desecularization"[11] and "unsecularization"[12] to describe this global tendency. One scholar who refers to this sea change as the "revenge of God" described it as a "new religious movement . . . aimed no longer at adapting to secular values but at recovering a sacred foundation for the organization of society—by changing society if necessary." He concluded, "Expressed in a multitude of ways, this approach advocated moving on from a modernism that had failed, attributing its setbacks and dead ends to separation from God."[13]

The process of globalization has accelerated the postmodern worldview which, in turn, has spurred the reaction of religious resurgence we are witnessing worldwide. As Samuel Huntington has noted, this "religious resurgence throughout the world is a reaction against secularism, moral relativism, and self-indulgence."[14]

The Loss of Meaning

The ancient religions of the world are growing in strength because people sense they are being absorbed into a way of life with no meaning. In a global, postmodern society, they see themselves running along a never-ending treadmill of credit spending and consumption or becoming trapped in the dead end of poverty. They sense the transience of life, and the global society draws them into a social world that may well be defined as living "within the context of no context."[15] For a growing number of youth throughout the world, "pop culture provides the matrix that contains much of what counts as 'meaning.'"[16] Many of the Western world's residents are losing a sense of permanence on all fronts. The functions of media, advertising, shopping, and entertainment consumption tempt us to devote our lives to that which is trivial.

It is correctly said that he who controls the story controls the culture. A litmus test to determine who controls a story of a people is the calendar. He who controls the calendar controls the story. In America, the autumn brings new television series; the summer is the blockbuster season for movies. Media, fashions, seasonal sports together confuse things by cutting them off from the past, reducing the calendar of holidays to mean nothing more than to pursue the promoted agendas of having "fun" for the sake of fun. Social memory is being dulled and is being replaced with media memory, which is no memory at all!

Recently a sober observer of our plight pointed out, "And if there were more people on the face of the earth who understood Nietzsche in 1957 than there had been in 1890, what did that mean in the face of television—or rock and roll? Once again, people are ritual- and truth-hungry. Once again, they have no sense of the sequence in which the cultural objects they are in reference to took their shape."[17] This is a harrowing truth upon which evangelical Christians should reflect if they are to grasp the task that lies before them in constructing sound biblical theology for the twenty-first century. We dare not seek to satisfy this growing desire for ritual and truth at the expense of forsaking the fundamentals of the faith. To do so would be to offer a Christianity that is just another product for the moment, without any eternal value or consequence.

An Interrupted Society

The uncertainty produced by this absence of profound or real meaning rather than popular meaning is compounded by the unexpected increase in the experience of interruption. Beepers and cell phones allow others to seize one's situation. Messages also come quickly by E-mail; in the case of instant messaging, they are as fast as the phone. And with handheld computing devices, known as personal digital assistants (or affectionately as PDAs), these messages are as portable as cell phones. Being unavailable is becoming inexcusable.

Meanwhile, the tyranny of flexibility is turning a growing number of fathers and mothers into contingent workers, temporary workers, and postmodern migrant workers. Career changes, training time, and retooling are on the increase among adults, right along with attention deficit syndrome among the young. The home has become a temporary base of operations. A just-in-time lifestyle makes everyone a fading memory in a fast-paced life.

The older order of corporate stability and career loyalty has passed from the scene. Longevity has increased, but career value has dropped. The age of fifty no longer announces arrival into the upper ranks of status and achievement; rather it signifies the fear of running in the workplace to escape from predators half one's age.

Peter Drucker, a master analyst of corporate life, has noted that "every existing society, even the most individualistic one, takes two things for granted, if only subconsciously: (1) organizations outlive workers, and (2) most people stay put. But today the opposite is true. The need to manage oneself is therefore creating a revolution in human affairs."[18] The social force of globalization serves as an institutional solvent, dissolving fixed institutional life into a new and highly flexible situation. It no longer seems possible to obtain a sense of certainty from without. "Nowadays, if there is any certainty in our lives, it comes increasingly from within rather than from without: You have to manage yourself rather than waiting for other people to do the managing."[19] The new global person is being forced to steer herself into her own future via her own Palm Pilot.

THE NATURE OF OUR GOSPEL

For our part, we confess God does not dispense His grace to His people and leave them to inhabit a vacuum of either understanding or duty. We are evangelical Christians. God has allotted to us the faith to *proclaim* the gospel. *The gospel is the good news* that announces what God has done for us sinners through His Christ, and that He requires of us faith in His Son for our salvation, according to the Scriptures. Those who embrace nihilistic rhetoric demand censorship of this good news because of its exclusive nature. We must disobey. We must prove that Nietzsche and his followers are wrong. Relativism is the wrong response to the new conditions of life we face.

We must not be deceived. The message of the gospel will cause others anguish and pain. It will provoke anger and produce misunderstanding toward followers of Christ. This suffering of insult and shame in turn will result in Christians being stigmatized, condemned, and persecuted. We must preach it anyway.

We must also realize that we will be tempted to preach the gospel for the wrong reasons and with the wrong emphasis. We may preach it to justify ourselves. We may be tempted to preach the gospel in triumphant terms, in sentimental terms, in terms of temporary relief or even as an item of head-nodding or foot-tapping entertainment. Each of these is an exercise in evil rhetoric—a style of communication that upholds the order of the status quo instead of overturning the powers of evil, which rule this world. As David Toole has observed, "To tell the good news without sap is a difficult thing."[20] On a comparative basis we do well to consider what one novelist admits, "It is a risky enterprise to have to write of virtue."[21] Our task should include guarding the gospel from being understood as trite, hackneyed, ridiculously sentimental, or ludicrously trivial. We should strive to achieve this with the same degree of diligence we would devote to maintaining doctrinal soundness.

Here again, holding on to the fundamentals of the faith and taking them to heart will help us. We preach the mystery that the suffering of death is meaningful. We carry the tragedy of death in us, but we go beyond the tragic in our dealing with it. We admit that, in natural terms, the tragic bears noble witness to the glory and mystery of what it means to be a human being. Nonetheless, we know, we confess, we proclaim that this is not enough. To be human means to be made in the image of God and to be called to bear that image to God's glory.

We must preach the gospel, anticipating that some will condemn our frontal assault as more than futile or absurd. They will label us disruptive and abusive. Nevertheless, we are called to live out lives of "revolutionary subordination." According to theologian John Howard Yoder, "Subordination means the acceptance of an *order,* as it exists, but with the new meaning given to it by the fact that one's acceptance of it is willing and meaningfully motivated."[22]

Our calling is not to perform "strategic calculus" in attempts at getting the right handle on the course of history and "move it in the right direction." Yoder wisely points out, "Is there not in Christ's teaching on meekness, or in the attitude of Jesus toward power and servanthood, a . . . question being raised about whether it is our business at all to guide our action by the course we wish history to take?"[23] To confess Christ calls us to set down the politics of effectiveness and to take up the politics of the cross. This is not defeatist or utopic, nor is it pragmatic or merely an act of obedience. Rather it is a matter of understanding ourselves in light of the work that God is doing in the world. It demands that we take part in that work, thus seeing ourselves as working with the grain of the universe as the Lord laid it out. This is the highest calling imaginable. As evangelical Christians, we have the opportunity to take up this way of life. Clearly, those who want to live like this need good theology.

THE FUNDAMENTALS OF THE FAITH

The Inerrant Scriptures

Such a theology is built upon the foundation of the fundamentals of the faith. Biblical inerrancy, the virgin birth of Jesus, the doctrine of substitutionary atonement, and the bodily resurrection and physical return of Christ are the bedrock upon which all evangelical theology and practice must be grounded.

Among these, biblical inerrancy understandably serves as the cornerstone of evangelical theology. Inerrancy is a way of saying we have confidence in the Scriptures and that we take them to be reliable and authoritative. The term *inerrant,* meaning "without error," requires our subordination to the Scriptures in the ordering of our lives within a modern cultural context. The Scriptures originated with the Holy Spirit, were written by men, were recognized and received by the church following the ministry of our Lord under the care of His appointed apostles, and were borne witness to in the life of the church by the Holy Spirit.

We confess that the Scriptures are reliable and without error. At the same time, we must also admit that our own theological communication of this truth is not infallible and thus must be open to question and subject to refinement and clarification. Nonetheless, even as we do this, we depend solely upon the Scriptures and avail ourselves of the renewing and transforming work of the Holy Spirit. We do so with the confidence we gain by reading the Word of our Lord recorded in Scripture that, "He who believes in Me, as the Scripture said, 'From his innermost being will flow rivers of living water'" (John 7:38 NASB). We bear this message to the world and especially to the church universal outside the community of evangelical Christianity.

Scripture is the final arbiter in all matters of life and death and faith and truth. In an interdependent age of chaos such as ours today, the authority of Scripture may serve as a source of strength and comfort in understanding our world, as well as a means of checking the religious claims of others.

Postmodernism has unleashed a legion of voices and a litany of conflicting agendas. The words of William Tyndale, a champion of translating the Scriptures into English in the sixteenth century, remain equally relevant for us today: "In so great diversity of spirits how shall I know who lieth and who saith truth? Whereby shall I try them and judge them?" We echo his response, "Verily by God's word which only is true. But how shall I do that when thou wilt not let me see the scripture?"[24] We want people to see the Scripture and rest in its authority as a warrant for claims of truth made about the name of Jesus. We want people to examine the Scripture with eagerness and regularity so that they will know whether the things we have said are indeed so.

The Virgin Birth

Because the Scriptures are inerrant, our primary concern when it comes to the doctrine of the virgin birth of Jesus need not be to defend this truth. Nor should we attempt to prove it. When the early church compiled the story of Jesus, it simply reported this fact as a part of what happened. It is naive to think that such a testimony about the birth of Jesus would not have been problematic in the first century. If left to an anonymous redactor's judgment, based upon what would avoid controversy, perhaps this portion of the account about Jesus' birth would have been edited out. We read scant little of the Lord's birth in the rest of the New Testament. The story of the Virgin Birth did, indeed, prompt scorn and ridicule among hostile critics of the Christian movement. Why then did it remain in the Gospels of Matthew and Luke?

The virgin birth of Jesus is included in the Gospels because the apostles knew it to be true and said so.

The divine nature of the Lord Jesus Christ is absolute. It is not simply unique; it is exclusive. His standing as Lord and Savior condemns as unqualified all others who might claim to mediate between God and man. Jesus Christ is the only one qualified to be our mediator because He alone has the ability to save sinners as well as the desire to do so. He shows divine love for sinners by having given Himself on the cross as a ransom for all. No one else was equal to the task.

His divine standing is universal. He is, as the creed of Nicea declares, "true God of true God" over all of humankind.

We believe that only a divine witness can ultimately prove the claims of a divine person. Nevertheless we must have the courage to warn others that to deny the deity of Christ endangers their eternal souls. When we preach the gospel, we commend our listeners into the hands of the God-man, Jesus Christ, confident that He knows each of us best and loves each one with a just and perfect love.

Substitutionary Atonement

If, however, the inerrancy of Scripture is the crux of evangelical theology, then the doctrine of substitutionary atonement is the crux of the evangelical gospel. It is primarily through this demonstration of God's love that the Lord Jesus reveals His identity: "For even the Son of Man did not come to be served, but to serve, and to give his life as a ransom for many" (Mark 10:45). Jesus declared Himself to be one sent by God according to prophecy that the Scripture might be fulfilled (John 19:24, 28, 36–37).

Many things may be said about Jesus, but if these things are said without announcing the shedding of blood for forgiveness of sin, then we preach a different gospel—one that is without power (Eph. 1:7; Heb. 9:22; 1 Peter 1:18–19). We might remain counted as "Christian" in the ranks of religion, but we have abandoned the living faith.

The Resurrection and Return of Christ

The atonement demonstrates the depth of God's love for sinners. The truth of the Resurrection testifies to the promise and the power of God. Death, the final enemy, has been defeated. One day it will be abolished, being swallowed up in the victory won for us by our Lord (1 Cor. 15:26, 54–57). The Resurrection is a historical event. But it is also an event that anticipates the future; it points toward the day when all things will be summed up in Christ. This means that the doctrine of the bodily resurrection of Christ cannot be separated from the doctrine of the Second Coming. Christ's return will end the historical process.

This is an apocalyptic view, which is thoroughly rejected by contemporary culture. Evangelicals take what the Bible says about time, history, and prophecy seriously in a literal sense. We hold as a living hope that time serves God, being converted by Him into fulfilled prophecy according to His purposes as He promised. We believe quite simply that not only do individuals need a Savior, but also that history, left to solely human devices, is unable to provide one. The historical process itself is absent of a redemptive means or mechanism. Because of His loving-kindness, God has intervened by sending His Son to provide an effective and legitimate redemptive history.

This is a crucial message for people to hear in the twenty-first century. Too many have been deceived into believing that technology—material or therapeutic—is able to deliver us. In our preaching we urge people to consider the Lord's resurrection as proof for His making good on His promise that He has the power and desire to provide peace: "In the past God overlooked such ignorance, but now he commands all people everywhere to repent. For he has set a day when he will judge the world with justice by the man he has appointed. He has given proof of this to all men by raising him from the dead" (Acts 17:30–31). The Resurrection not only demonstrates the Father's approval of the Son's substitutionary death, it also points to His return!

The "blessed hope" of Christ's return gives men and women the confidence to invest in the future. This gift should not be underestimated. Failure to have faith in the future leads to either the paralysis of fatalism or the excesses of decadence. The Christianization of a culture exorcises it of fatalism, even as it temporizes its decadent tendencies.

THE CROSS OF REALITY

A thoughtful Christian thinker in the twentieth century, Eugen Rosenstock-Huessy (1888–1973), has provided us with a model, which he called "the cross of reality," to help us understand how to live in light of the fundamentals of the faith in our evangelical community.[25] The diagram on the following page has been adapted from his model.

We devote ourselves to promoting *peace* (see diagram, "The Cross of Reality") by the preaching and the living of the gospel within the world, among the various confessing communities of Christian faith, and especially among one another as evangelical Christians.[26] In this context, then, peace "is that experience

THE CROSS OF REALITY

Source: Adapted from Eugen Rosenstock-Huessy, *Speech and Reality* (Norwich, Vt.: Argo Books, 1970), 15–16.

of love and fellowship that offers the opportunity to listen."[27] The two ways we help others is through speech and service. In speaking the gospel we announce the salvation that God offers in His Son. By serving others we show others the nature of His love and how it has changed us. The peace we so seek is constantly under siege, in our own hearts, in our fellowship with one another, and with our relating to others outside of our fellowship. Maintenance of this peace requires that we concern ourselves with the two different ways we live out our daily lives, through the medium of time —our bearing responsibility for both our past and our future—and in the midst of the social reality of relations with those who live around us.

Crisis—the left side of the crossbeam on this cross of reality— represents the condition of disagreement within evangelical Christianity. Scripture teaches us how to be subject to one another.

Unanimity is a ministry nurtured through fellowship, admonishment, and encouragement. Beyond this, if we disagree over the essentials of the faith, then the very continuance of evangelicalism as a renewal movement within the church could be placed in jeopardy. Doctrinal unanimity too must be continuously nurtured. Each generation of evangelical Christians needs to grapple with issues about the fundamentals of the truth taken from Scripture as understood and communicated in the living moment. We do not do this only selfishly to mitigate our own uncertainties but in service to those who will come after us and in honor of those who carried the faith before us. Such an attitude of heart brings glory to our Lord.

At the other end of the crossbeam is the threat of *conflict*. This represents our relations with others outside of evangelicalism. We must guard against attacking others or hating others. We should be prepared to suffer shame for the name of Jesus, but we should not use this expectation as an excuse to stop sharing the story of Jesus or to stop serving those whom He loves. Peace is never a static condition. It is always an initiative and a moment in the life of a community lived out in relation to other contemporaneous social groups. Those committed to advancing peace communicate with others; they invite others to enter into an exchange of listening so that they may learn from one another.

Those projects of service that can be entered into in common while keeping one's own identity intact are done in partnership with one another. Those who agree to do this recognize two truths. First, a true peace initiative will call for taking action through serving others. Peace preached truthfully is practiced by doing real works of compassion, of ministering to those who hurt, who hate, or who need help. Second, to take up such service means to undergo the inescapable effects of change that happens through being involved in other peoples' lives over which we have no control. While taking up these challenges, we work to preserve unity among ourselves and struggle to resolve unnecessary conflict with others outside our community of faith.

This process of peace-building not only requires the ongoing response of listening and learning from one another, it also demands that we vigilantly protect and care for our own community of faith (Rom. 14:19). This points us to the vertical beam of the cross of reality, which represents a group's life in time. As evangelical Christians, we constantly face our past heritage and our future hope of being home with the Lord. The two should be transferred together from one generation to the next. But this is not a static exercise like passing a baton in a relay race. There are the twin threats of *decadence* and *revolution*. A decadent evangelical community would lose the conviction and enthusiasm needed to encourage the next generation to take up its vision and cause. A revolutionary evangelical community refusing to respect its own past would expose it to betrayal and abandonment. To what should we remain loyal in relation to our past? Before what should we keep the faith in our facing the future? We do not simply ask these questions as if posing an intellectual puzzle. We wrestle with them while our children watch us. How we answer them will determine the vantage point that the next generation will take as it embarks upon the same task.

If we allow ourselves to become overly absorbed in the present—the great temptation of this postmodern era—then we will live less of our lives in anticipation of the things to come. Our children will learn this from us. Without our saying a word, we will contribute to the dulling of the blessed hope held by the next generation of evangelical Christians. Similarly, we must carefully determine which of the doctrines we have received from our past demand our loyalty. How we cultivate our past will have enormous influence upon the next generation of evangelicals. Failure to respect the essentials of the faith will sow seeds that will later bear the fruit of their being rejected by those who follow after us.

Reliance upon the Scriptures to instruct us about the fundamentals of the faith is crucial to this practice of caring for our community of faith and our churches. We must not just believe them or communicate them correctly; we must live them out and carry them within us as qualities of character. We should be people who confess, "The sacred writings stand over us." We submit to Scripture and rely upon it for knowledge about life, ministry, teaching, and witness. We invite others to learn of Jesus. We invite them to discover who He is, what He has done, what He offers, and what He requires by examining the Scriptures. The fundamentals of the faith are precious living gems of truth about our Lord and Savior, which have come out of this storage house of treasure.

LIVING OUR CHRISTIAN HOPE

Perhaps this is the most important way for us to live out the Christian hope in this age. Let us not merely fight for the Bible; let us live by it. Let us live with it and live out our union with Christ under its authority. To do so will cause us to live in opposition to the temperament of this age. We live under the pressure of being caught in a cultural pincer movement between the "morality of historical knowledge," dictating acceptance of "standards of truth and honesty which have dominated the scholarly community since the Enlightenment,"[28] and a postmodern infatuation with the notion that myth has replaced the role of revelation as something that makes our lives meaningful. We suffer this crisis as old religious loyalties are being fanned back into life in part as a reaction to their experiencing the very same dilemma that we face. Under such circumstances, it is our challenge and blessing to bear witness to Christ and to live out our lives in pursuit of peace by serving others in His name. It is important for us to have a self-critical concern to judge our theology by our apostolic origins.

This exercise of reaching back to the Scriptures keeps us from forsaking the faith we have received. We must remain rooted in the Scriptures regularly and not by rote. Those who developed the fundamentals of the faith did so in a certain moment of cultural crisis brought about by the forces of modernism. Those forces are not spent but new social forces have arisen alongside them. They carried those fundamentals through the era of modernism. We need to carry them into the new cultural environment of the twenty-first century. We trust Him to do so to His glory.

Several years ago Moody Bible Institute President George Sweeting preached during a weekly chapel about Paul's life being threatened in Damascus. To Paul's rescue came the disciples, who "took him by night and let him down through an opening in the wall, lowering him in a large basket" (Acts 9:25 NASB). I remember the message; Dr. Sweeting stressed that not everyone is sent to be a missionary like Paul. Some of us, he said, are called to "hold the ropes," even as the disciples did then and thus allowed Paul to go on his way to be a missionary. He explained that some Christians are called to stay home and provide for missionaries through their prayers and by their financial support.

Urging his listeners to support missionaries, Sweeting called the church to action with a solid message of encouragement. I can still hear his voice, "So hold those ropes! Hold the ropes."

So, too, should we "hold the ropes" in remaining loyal to the essential truths of Christianity. Let us hold the ropes by remaining subject to the Scriptures as our source and authority for telling, teaching, transmitting, and testing the story of Jesus. Let us hold the ropes as we engage in theological reflection and attempt to build a healthy and correct Christian worldview that is based upon the Bible. Let us hold the ropes as we proclaim the fundamentals of the faith to our own generation. Finally, let us hold the ropes as we hand these precious gems of living truth down to the generation of evangelical Christians that comes after us for the purpose of serving Christ in the building of His church "ere He return."

NOTES

1. Hans Kung, *The Catholic Church,* trans. John Bowden (London: Phoenix Press, 2002), 130.
2. I have adapted these comments from the thought of the anthropologist and social thinker Ernest Becker. See his works *Denial of Death* and *Escape from Evil.*
3. Jacques Ellul, *Propaganda* (New York: Random, 1973), 31.
4. A pride anchored in religious faith practiced but not admitted. As Jose Ortega y Gasset noted, "Science is a faith, belief to which one subscribes just as one may subscribe to a religious belief"; *Man and Crisis,* trans. Mildred Adams (New York: Norton, 1958), 103.
5. Peter Watson, *The Modern Mind: An Intellectual History of the 20th Century* (New York: HarperCollins, 2001), 751, 772. Watson's book describes well the present condition and confession of science.
6. Francis Fukuyama, "Biotechnology and the Threat of a Posthuman Future," *The Chronicle of Higher Education,* sec. 2 (22 March 2002): B8.
7. Eugen Rosenstock-Huessy, *Out of Revolution: Autobiography of Western Man* (Norwich, Vt.: Argo Books, 1969), 738.
8. Malcolm Waters, *Globalization* (New York: Routledge, 1995), 3.
9. Ibid., 8.
10. Samuel P. Huntington, *The Clash of Civilizations and the Remaking of World Order* (New York: Simon & Schuster, 1996).
11. Peter L. Berger, ed., *Desecularization of the World: Resurgent Religion and World Politics* (Grand Rapids: Eerdmans, 1999). Berger also wrote an earlier challenge to the secularization thesis in 1970, *A Rumor of Angels: Modern Society and the Rediscovery of the Supernatural,* in which he assessed the manifestation of "religious politicization."
12. George Weigel, "Religion and Peace: An Argument Complexified," *Washington Quarterly* 14 (spring 1991): 27.
13. Gilles Kepel, *Revenge of God: The Resurgence of Islam, Christianity and Judaism in the Modern World,* trans. Alan Braly (University Park, Pa.: Pennsylvania State Univ., 1994), 2.
14. Huntington, *The Clash of Civilizations,* 98.
15. George W. S. Trow, *Within the Context of No Context* (New York: Atlantic Monthly Press, 1997).
16. Tom Beaudoin, *Virtual Faith* (San Francisco: Jossey-Bass, 1998), 22.
17. Trow, *Within the Context of No Context,* 29. I agree with Trow that "in America, it is dangerous to know very much—or *anything*" (p. 36).
18. Peter Drucker, "Managing Oneself," *Harvard Business Review,* March–April 1999; as cited in John Micklethwait and Adrian Wooldridge, *A Future Perfect* (New York: Crown, 2000), 326.
19. John Micklethwait and Adrian Wooldridge, *A Future Perfect: The Challenge and Hidden Promise of Globalization* (New York: Crown, 2001), 314.
20. David Toole, *Waiting for Godot in Sarajevo* (Boulder, Colo.: Westview, 1998), 263.
21. Thomas Keneally, *Schindler's List* (New York: Simon & Schuster, 1993), 14.
22. John Howard Yoder, *The Politics of Jesus,* 2d ed. (Grand Rapids: Eerdmans, 1994), 172.

23. Ibid., 228–30.
24. William Tyndale, *The Obedience of a Christian Man* (1528; reprint, London: Penguin Books, 2000), 20. At the time of his writing this under the 1408 "Constitutions of Oxford," the "translating, owning, or reading a Bible in English was forbidden, and severely punishable—including by being burned alive" (p. 202).
25. Klaus-Gunter Wesseling, "Rosenstock-Huessy," *Biographisch-Bibliographisches Kirchenlexikon* 8 (1994): 688–95.
26. Evangelical Christianity is made up of a diverse number of different faith communities. See Robert Weber, *Common Roots* (Grand Rapids: Zondervan, 1978), for an overview of evangelical groupings.
27. Eugen Rosenstock-Huessy, *Speech and Reality* (Norwich, Vt.: Argo Books, 1970), 36–37.
28. Van A. Harvey, *The Historian and the Believer: The Morality of Historical Knowledge and Christian Belief* (Philadelphia: Westminster, 1966), 246.

Michael McDuffee is professor of theology at the Moody Bible Institute. He earned a Ph.D. degree from Brandeis University, Waltham, Massachusetts, and holds academic degrees from the University of New Hampshire and Wheaton Graduate School, Wheaton, Illinois.

SINCE 1894, Moody Publishers has been dedicated to equip and motivate people to advance the cause of Christ by publishing evangelical Christian literature and other media for all ages, around the world. Because we are a ministry of the Moody Bible Institute of Chicago, a portion of the proceeds from the sale of this book go to train the next generation of Christian leaders.

If we may serve you in any way in your spiritual journey toward understanding Christ and the Christian life, please contact us at www.moodypublishers.com.

"All Scripture is God-breathed and is useful for teaching, rebuking, correcting and training in righteousness, so that the man of God may be thoroughly equipped for every good work."
—2 TIMOTHY 3:16, 17

MOODY
PUBLISHERS

THE NAME YOU CAN TRUST®

FOUNDATIONAL FAITH TEAM

ACQUIRING EDITOR:
Mark Tobey

COPY EDITOR:
Jim Vincent

BACK COVER COPY:
Julie-Allyson Ieron, Joy Media

COVER DESIGN:
Ragont Design

INTERIOR DESIGN:
Ragont Design

PRINTING AND BINDING:
Versa Press Incorporated

The typeface for the text of this book is
Sabon